KAFKA

A BEGINNER'S GUIDE

STEVE COOTS

Series Editors
Rob Abbott & Charlie Bell

Hodder & Stoughton

A MEMBER OF THE HODDER HEADLINE GROUP

Family and for Lucie

Orders: please contact Bookpoint Ltd, 130 Milton Park, Abingdon, Oxon OX14 4SB. Telephone:
(44) 01235 827720, Fax: (44) 01235 400554. Lines are open from 9.00–6.00, Monday to Saturday,
with a 24-hour message answering service. Email address: orders@bookpoint.co.uk

British Library Cataloguing in Publication Data
A catalogue record for this title is available from The British Library

ISBN 0 340 84648 8

First published 2002
Impression number   10 9 8 7 6 5 4 3 2 1
Year   2007 2006 2005 2004 2003 2002

Cover photo from Bettman/Corbis.
Typeset by Transet Limited, Coventry, England.
Printed in Great Britain for Hodder & Stoughton Educational, a division of Hodder Headline
Plc, 338 Euston Road, London NW1 3BH by Cox & Wyman, Reading, Berks.

CONTENTS

How to use this book

The *Beginner's Guide* series aims to introduce readers to major writers of the past 500 years. It is assumed that readers will begin with little or no knowledge and will want to go on to explore the subject in other ways.

BEGIN READING THE AUTHOR

This book is a companion guide to Kafka's major works; it is not a substitute for reading the books themselves. It would be useful if you read some of the works in parallel, so that you can put theory into practice. This book is divided into sections. After considering how to approach the author's work and a brief biography, we go on to explore some of Kafka's main writings and themes before examining some critical approaches to the author. The survey finishes with suggestions for further reading and possible areas of further study.

HOW TO APPROACH UNFAMILIAR OR DIFFICULT TEXTS

Coming across a new writer may seem daunting, but do not be put off. The trick is to persevere. Much good writing is multi-layered and complex. It is precisely this diversity and complexity which makes literature rewarding and exhilarating.

Literary work often needs to be read more than once, and in different ways. These ways can include: a leisurely and superficial reading to get the main ideas and narrative; a slower more detailed reading focusing on the nuances of the text, concentrating on what appear to be key passages; and reading in a random way, moving back and forth through the text to examine such things as themes, or narrative or characterization.

In complex texts it may be necessary to read in short chunks. When it comes to tackling difficult words or concepts it is often enough to guess in context on the first reading, making a more detailed study using a dictionary or book of critical concepts on later reading. If you prefer to look up unusual words as you go along, be careful that you do not disrupt the flow of the text and your concentration.

VOCABULARY

You will see that keywords and unfamiliar words are set in **bold** text. These words are defined and explained in the glossary to be found at the back of the book.

The book is a tool to help you appreciate a key figure in literature. We hope you enjoy reading it and find it useful.

✹ ✹ ✹ *SUMMARY* ✹ ✹ ✹

To maximize the use of this book:

- read Kafka's work;

- read it several times in different ways;

- be open to innovative or unusual forms of writing;

- persevere.

Why Read Franz Kafka Today?

> The one artist that I feel could be my brother – and I almost don't like
> saying it because the reaction is always, 'Yeah, you and everybody else'
> – is Franz Kafka.

D. Lynch, (Ed. C. Rodley), *Lynch on Lynch*, (Faber and Faber 1997), p56.

How has a clerk in an insurance firm in Prague at the beginning of the
twentieth century captured so many people's imagination? In his
lifetime Kafka had only a handful of short stories published, he never
exclusively involved himself in literary circles, his novels were not
finished and he wanted his work destroyed after his death.

An initial search on the Internet, however, will provide over 30,000
websites with links to the author. According to the playwright Alan
Bennett: 'His work has been garrisoned by armies of critics with some
15,000 books about him at the last count.' (A. Bennett, *Alan Bennett:
Plays 2*, (Faber and Faber 1998), p3). Further to this, the critic Martin
Seymour-Smith boldly states that Kafka '…has been both more widely
influential and more widely interpreted than any other single modern
writer. If he is not the supreme prose writer of the century, then he is
among the two or three who are.' (M. Seymour-Smith, *Guide to
Modern World Literature*, (Papermac 1986), p609.)

So, why all the fuss?

EXTERNALIZING THE DEMONS

Kafka's work explores the turmoil of someone lost in a world of fear,
guilt and confusion. We need only look at how our modern language
has developed formal labels for these concerns to see how Kafka relates
to our contemporary society: 'the dysfunctional family', 'Post-
Traumatic Stress Syndrome' and 'Human Rights' to name but a few.

Kafka's work has become a symbol for those who are battling against the unseen – whether it is external authority or internal confusion. The opening of *The Trial* sums this up perfectly. 'Someone must have been telling lies about Joseph K., for without having done anything wrong he was arrested one fine morning.' (F. Kafka (trans. W and E Muir), *The Trial*, p7.)

His writing casts a critical eye over any society that uses authority as a means of control – from parents to government. Kafka caricatures this authority as an oppressor capable of total destruction as, for example, here where the once benign rocks, representing overseeing authority, turn upon the narrator: '…I fell and in a moment I was torn and transpierced by the sharp rocks which had always gazed up at me so peacefully from the rushing water.' (F. Kafka (trans. W. and E. Muir), *The Bridge, The Penguin Complete Short Stories*, p412.)

CAPTURING UNIVERSAL FEAR

Kafka's writing grows beyond his personal experience and becomes relevant to the world in general. This is why he has been adopted by so many ideological and philosophical thinkers. Jewish academics have taken Kafka as an emblem of the persecution of their culture, existentialist thinkers recognize in him the struggle of identity and, on the political side, he represents the struggle of the dispossessed against a totalitarian authority.

In the opening of *The Castle*, for instance, we can perceive an unknown, oppressive power creating the feeling of a David confronting his Goliath.

> The Castle hill was hidden, veiled in mist and darkness, nor was there even a glimmer of light to show that a castle was there. On the wooden bridge leading from the main road to the village K. stood for a long time gazing into the illusory emptiness above him.

> F. Kafka, *The Castle*, p9

A LONG JOURNEY TO RECOGNITION

It took a long time, but now Kafka is regarded as a major figure, not only in the study of literature, but also in the study of European society and history as well as Judaism. Just as George Orwell gave us the word '**Orwellian**', so Kafka too has become an adjective. 'Kafkaesque' is commonplace in our language, referring to 'man's fear, isolation and bewilderment in a nightmarish dehumanized world'. (*Collins English Dictionary*, (Collins 1986), p531.)

> **KEYWORDS**
>
> Orwellian: Referring to a dehumanized, authoritarian society as described in the novel *1984*.
>
> Parable: A story that uses familiar events to portray a religious or ethical situation.

KAFKA TODAY

With the hindsight of recent history, especially in terms of the changes in Eastern Europe at the end of the twentieth century, we can see how Kafka was, more by accident than design, a supreme commentator of the social turmoil of his country and community. His work, being so fantastic, gives us modern **parables** by which we can keep in mind how dangerous and ridiculous our world can become.

The critic Martin Esslin, in his book about the Theatre of the Absurd, comments that the works of Kafka '…have become the supreme expression of the situation of modern man'. (M. Esslin, *The Theatre of the Absurd*, p355). Alan Bennett, who wrote the play *Kafka's Dick*, loosely based on Kafka's life, says: 'His work prefigures the future, often in ways that are both specific and dreadful and this is part of his popular reputation.' (Alan Bennett, *Alan Bennett: Plays 2*, (Faber and Faber 1998), pviii.)

Kafka's work remains in print and continues to inspire writers, artists and film makers. Indeed, the very title of Frederick Karl's weighty biography of Kafka, points to Kafka's new status: *Franz Kafka, Representative Man. Prague, Germans, Jews, and the Crisis of Modernism*. In the preface of the book Karl goes on to explain: 'The greatness of Franz Kafka is that he forces us to rethink everything we take for granted.' (F. Karl, *Franz Kafka, Representative Man*, pxvi.)

Kafka's work has finally started to escape from the Prague ghetto of its creation to the point where he is being embraced by the city that once reviled him. In the tourist areas it is almost impossible to move without coming across sellers of Kafka T-shirts and mugs. Kafka is a regular figure in Czech waxwork museums and there are plenty of societies, cafés and bookshops linked to his name.

As long as we have faceless authority lurking in the shadows, fear and guilt gnawing away inside and confusion about our world, we will always have Kafka. He is read today because he documented the struggle to understand the absurdity of authority and society.

❋ ❋ ❋ SUMMARY ❋ ❋ ❋

- Kafka's work explores many of today's social and emotional concerns.

- The term 'Kafkaesque' has come to symbolize the individual struggling in a nightmare world.

- His work reflects the 'everyman' in relation to the oppressed and fearful.

- After many years in the wilderness, Kafka is now openly embraced by the city of Prague, the Czech Republic and Eastern Europe.

How to Approach Kafka's Work

BE WARY OF THE DECEPTIVE SHADOWS

The work of Kafka is wrapped in dark shadows and gloomy atmospheres. He can be seen as a joyless writer obsessed with the negative aspects of life – helplessness, guilt and the fear of not being understood.

When approaching Kafka's work it is indeed easy to react to his writing with this bleak feeling dominating the enjoyment of the storytelling. The situations in which he places his characters are indeed grim and unforgiving, but they are also absurd and he caricatures the social systems with which his heroes have to struggle. Kafka turns the world into a grotesque joke.

LETTING IN THE HUMOUR

Although Kafka was a writer who tapped into his own fear and self-loathing, eventually his paranoia breaks into a brutal hilarity. Humour exploits self-depreciation and that element of humour is strong in the Jewish community. Humour *is* evident in Kafka's work, although not in an obvious way. Indeed, it is usually missed altogether because it is buried beneath his overtly black vision of the world. The tragedy in Kafka's work can easily topple over into comedy albeit one born of the gallows, as when Joseph K., in *The Trial*, has to deal with his bed-ridden advocate. As Alan Bennett comments: '*The Trial*, for instance, is a much funnier book than it has got credit for and Kafka's jokes about himself are better for the desperate circumstances in which they were often made.' (A. Bennett, *Alan Bennett: Plays 2*, Faber and Faber 1998, p5.)

TRADITIONAL STORYTELLING

Kafka was born into the heart of the Jewish community of Eastern Europe which has a strong tradition of storytelling. This helped shape

Kafka's approach to writing. The story of the **Golem**, for instance, was particularly intriguing for him. In effect, what Kafka did was write adult fairy tales, using the symbols and iconography of his contemporary world to tell tales and **allegories** that would relate to every generation.

NON-TRADITIONAL STORYTELLING

But, be careful. Kafka's work does not manifest as straightforward storytelling. It is easy to be disappointed by his work if you are expecting a linear narrative approach. With his major works, Kafka looks to explore and expand a central idea. Martin Greenberg explains:

> [Kafka's] narrative art lies in the elaboration, the unfolding of a basic image, rather than in the traditional representation of an action. The Kafka story is not dramatic but visionary; it does not move from beginning to the middle to the end of an action, it progresses through intensities of seeing toward an ever deeper vision.
>
> M. Greenberg (ed. H. Bloom), *Modern Critical Views: Kafka*, p68

So don't expect fiery, action-packed denouements with Kafka. *The Castle*, for instance, peters out, and *The Trial* ends with a low-key, muddy execution.

DARK IMAGES

What mostly sticks in the memory after reading a piece by Kafka is the sinister imagery he employs to tell his tales. Characters are arrested for no reason, sombre gothic castles overshadow villages, starving

---

KEYWORDS

Golem: The traditional Jewish tale of a man made out of clay that was brought to life by a Rabbi to protect the community. The Yiddish word EMETH ('truth') is inscribed on the Golem's forehead to bring him to life (or written on parchment and placed in the Golem's mouth, depending on which version you read). Every Sabbath, the E is scratched off. The resultant word METH ('death') halts the Golem.

One Sabbath the Rabbi forgets to do this and the Golem runs amok, almost annihilating the community. The Rabbi arrives and rubs away the writing thus destroying the Golem. He then teaches the community to beware – that which protects can also destroy.

Allegory: A story, poem or picture in which the apparent meaning of the characters or events relate to a deeper or spiritual meaning.

side-show attractions waste away and travelling salesmen are transformed into gigantic insects.

Kafka had a rampant imagination and a clear motorway into his subconscious. He tapped his paranoia for his creative energy and gave a solid reality to his deepest fears. It is these images and exploration of the situations rather than strongly developed and crafted narratives that have established Kafka as a major writer.

FRAGMENTED WORK

When reading Kafka's writing it is important to keep in mind that the majority of his work was never fully finished. Most of it was published after his death having been pieced together by Max Brod, his friend and eventually editor, from the scraps Kafka left behind. Kafka wrote for the sake of writing rather than completing stories as a 'professional' author would. As Harold Bloom says: 'His longer narratives – *Amerika, The Trial,* even *The Castle* – are better in parts than as complete works; and his longer stories, even *The Metamorphosis,* begin more acutely than they tend to close.' (H. Bloom, *The Western Canon,* p448.)

KEY TERM

Aphorism: A short, pithy saying expressing a general truth.

Much of Kafka's work appears as small fragments and ideas as with *Reflections on Sin, Pain, Hope and the True Way,* a collection of 109 ideas and **aphorisms**. Again, this directs the reader to see that the value of Kafka's work is to be found in moments, isolated incidents and musings.

OTHER WRITING

As well as his fiction, Kafka was a great diarist and letter writer. The diaries and letters act to support and inform his fictional writing. In a way, Kafka's fiction can be seen as an extension to these letters and diaries. The letters are outward communications, the diaries act as a hub and the fiction works as an internal communication.

Kafka's three writing worlds were almost indistinguishable.

These elements of Kafka's writing cannot be read completely in isolation as they cross-fertilize each other. Kafka *was* his writing, not in an autobiographical sense but in a way of trying to give meaning to his world. When his fiction is seen in this way the troublesome weak endings, the fragments and the sense of incompleteness begin to sit more comfortably with the reader.

✳ ✳ ✳ *SUMMARY* ✳ ✳ ✳

● Although Kafka's fictional world was a dark, menacing place it can also be viewed as an absurd and humorous caricature.

● Kafka's narratives were rarely finished. The beauty of his writing is to be found in fragments, incidents and moments.

● Kafka explored and expanded a central idea in his work rather than working with the more traditional linear narrative.

● Kafka wrote diaries and letters as much as fiction. These three forms of writing link together and inform and support each other. Kafka *was* his writing and vice versa.

Biography and Influences 3

'WHAT VILLAGE IS THIS I HAVE WANDERED INTO?'

Franz Kafka was born in Prague on 3 July 1883. He was the first child of German-speaking Czech Jews, Herman and Julie Kafka. Their next two children were boys but they died in infancy. Three daughters followed; Elli (Gabrielle) in 1889, Valli (Valerie) in 1890 and Ottla (Ottilie) in 1892. Kafka remained close to his sisters throughout his lifetime, specifically Ottla.

Herman Kafka was very much a self-made man. He had come to Prague as a travelling salesman and set up his own shop on the Old Town square selling novelty goods, hardware, haberdashery and umbrellas. He built up the business through hard work and long hours. His wife would be there at his beck and call helping to make the business a success.

Kafka had little contact with his working parents, being brought up mainly by nurses. Indeed his early, pre-school years presented the infant writer with the upheavals of five moves of house because of his father's '…greed for prestige and respectability' (R. Hayman, *K: A Biography of Kafka*, p12). Although his mother was a loving woman, albeit under the shadow of her husband, it was his father who would prove to be a defining character in Kafka's life.

HERMAN VS FRANZ

All his life Franz was overshadowed by the figure of his powerful and extraordinarily imposing father.

M. Brod, *Franz Kafka*, p4

Kafka's father was very much a patriarch. He was hard-working to the point of martyrdom, very self-confident (to the outside world at least) and domineering to the point of bullying. He was everything that Kafka wasn't. Although loving and proud of his first and only surviving son, he appears to have been an awkward parent.

> So far as Kafka could remember his father never read to him, but taught him how to march, how to salute and how to sing military songs, let him drink beer, tried to encourage him with shouting, hand-clapping, mimicry and laughter, which no doubt seemed more unsympathetic than it was, and all these efforts to give the boy more confidence had the opposite effect.

R. Hayman, *K: A Biography of Kafka*, p12

This was an appalling environment for a boy as sensitive as Kafka.

Herman dominated the household and established strict codes of behaviour. Later, Kafka raged against him in *Letter to Father*, written in 1919, where he rebukes his father's dictatorship and hypocrisy.

Kafka struggled with his father's domination.

The main thing was that the bread be cut straight; but that you did it with a knife dripping with gravy was immaterial. We had to pay attention not to let any scraps fall onto the floor, in the end most of the scraps were under you. At the table we were only allowed to eat, but you cleaned and clipped your fingernails, sharpened pencils, cleaned your ears with a toothpick. Please understand me correctly, Father: in themselves these would have been utterly insignificant details, they only become depressing for me because you, the towering authoritative person for me, never held yourself to the commandments you imposed on me.

F. Kafka, *Letter to Father*, p20

Kafka and his father never resolved their differences.

SCHOOL, UNIVERSITY AND RESPECTABILITY

Practically the whole of Kafka's life revolved around Prague. As Kafka said:

Here was my secondary school, over there in that building facing us was the university, and a little further to the left, my office. My whole life' – and he drew a few small circles with his finger – 'is confined to this small circle.

H. Salfellner, *Franz Kafka and Prague*, p34

Kafka's elementary school, Deutsche Volks und Bürgerschule, was on the Old Town square, just across the way from his home. In 1893, Kafka attended the German Secondary school, Staatsgymnasium, also on the Old Town square. It was regarded as the strictest school in Prague. Kafka's father had chosen it because it had a good reputation for increasing the chances of work in the Imperial and Royal civil service. That is if the young Kafka was not to inherit his father's hard-earned business.

Kafka was a good pupil, well above average in his lessons (apart from maths) and mixed well with his contemporaries. After his schooling Kafka enrolled in the Deutsche Universität in 1901 to study law. Again, he was a good student, mixing well with the sons of the German bureaucracy and the intellectual Jewish middle class. It was here that he met Max Brod, who would become his life-long friend and the eventual editor of his work.

Mixing with the intellectuals of the university, Kafka grew into his writing and his need to write. It was here that he started his diaries. This set into process the schism that haunted Kafka for most of his life – the struggle between living the life of a writer and leading a respectable, middle-class life with a good job, wife and children – all the things that could make his father proud of him. This would not be easy as Kafka said himself: 'God doesn't want me to write, but I…I must.' (K. J. Fickert, *Franz Kafka. Life, Work and Criticism*, p23.)

A GOOD JOB WITH PROSPECTS

After graduating from university, Kafka, with a Doctor of Law Degree under his belt, obtained his first job with the insurance company Assicurazioni Generali on Wenceslas Square in Prague. The hours were long, frequently starting at 8.00 in the morning and not finishing until 8.30 in the evening. The pay was also poor and Kafka looked to move on.

In 1908 he secured a job with the Arbiter-Unfall-Versicherungs-Anstalt für das Königreich Böhmen (Worker's Accident Insurance Company for the Kingdom of Bohemia). He stayed with this company for 14 years until he was retired due to ill health. Kafka started as a temporary clerk, but over the years rose through the ranks to Secretary.

COMPULSIVE WRITING

In a letter to his fiancée's father in 1913, Kafka wrote: 'My whole existence is bound up with literature; this direction in my life I have maintained up to my thirtieth year. If I once abandon it, I simply shall not continue to live.' (K. J. Fickert, *Franz Kafka. Life, Work and Criticism*, p7.)

As a child, Kafka had an interest in theatre, specifically after the opening of the Neue Deutsche Theatre in 1888 and the arrival of a small **Yiddish** theatre troupe from Poland. Then, mixing with the intellectuals at

KEY TERM

Yiddish: Vernacular language spoken by European and emigrant Jews.

university, his eyes were opened to literature and he used to spend long hours with his friends discussing literature in the cafés around Prague. But, as was his wont, Kafka preferred to sit and observe more than he participated.

KEY TERM

Prague Castle and St Vitas' Cathedral: The castle and cathedral overlook Prague from the opposite side of the river Vltava. The buildings tower over the landscape and are one of the distinctive landmarks in the city.

Working during the day at the insurance company meant that Kafka had to write at night. Because he spent most of his time living in a disruptive environment at home he had to concentrate himself into total immersion with his writing. Even when he did rent his own flat, living in the city still proved to be too noisy. A solution came with the renting of a small house on Golden Lane in the shadow of **Prague Castle and St. Vitas' Cathedral**. Here he would write for the night and then walk back to his flat in town in the small hours.

WOMEN, WOMEN, WOMEN

Apart from his relationships with his sisters, Kafka's life was not blessed with successful relationships with women. When he did get involved, the relationships became more of an outlet for his letter writing.

The social placing of his family meant that one day he would be wed. Initially, Kafka regarded the notion of marriage as a means of escaping his father. He also thought that to '…have a wife who knew him and supported him from every angle would be like having God – having the possibility of loving approval from outside' (R. Hayman, *K: A Biography of Kafka*, p198).

Later in life, he felt instead the need to be rescued from the notion of marriage altogether. In a way, Kafka was more concerned with a romantic, unattainable love. Besides that, for Kafka, '…sex was connected to disgust, and that in turn to forms of dissolution, disintegration, even death. Sex was rarely something freely enjoyed.' (F. Karl, *Franz Kafka, Representative Man*, p142.)

Possibly this is again connected with his father, who thought sex was 'filthy', and the idea of his tyrant father in sexual congress with his mother was repugnant for Kafka.

Kafka never did marry although he was engaged three times – twice to the same woman, Felice Bauer. He got engaged to Bauer in 1914, breaking with her in the same year. The second engagement was in 1917. He, again, broke up with her soon after. During the romance he wrote hundreds of letters to her, even though their time together, physically, was brief.

In 1918, Kafka met Julie Wohryzek, the owner of a millinery shop, and proposed to her. This engagement was short lived after he met Milena Jesenká-Polak. Although Milena was married, she and Kafka struck up a strong friendship. Again, Kafka wrote her hundreds of letters. Kafka, despite being strongly attracted to Milena, viewed the relationship more as a literary one, eventually entrusting his journals to her.

His last significant female friendship was with the 19-year-old Dora Diamant. He met her in 1923 in the Baltic Spa of Müritz where he was on holiday. It seemed he had found happiness with her and they moved to Berlin together. The relationship became serious and they planned to move to Tel Aviv. For the first time, Kafka seemed to have found happiness in a relationship. But Kafka's illness was to bring an end to those dreams.

ILLNESS

Kafka had been pronounced as suffering with **tuberculosis** in 1917. Kafka was forever anxious about his health and had a lifelong friendship with illness, imagined or otherwise. He was obsessed with his slight frame and the neurosis of being weak beside his stout father who glowed with health. He was also sensitive to noise and was disgusted

KEY TERM

Tuberculosis: A communicable disease caused by *tubercle bacillus*. Most frequently attacks the lungs. Also known as consumption.

by the functions of the body. Yet despite Kafka's own view on his general health, the truth was the opposite. The health report from his first job concludes: 'He is a delicate but healthy man.' (S. Gilman, *Franz Kafka, The Jewish Patient*, p42.)

Throughout his life Kafka manifested his inner turmoil as minor physical ailments but he saw his tuberculosis as a 'triumph of his mental over his physical self, of the artist over the efficient bureaucrat, prospective husband, and dutiful son' (K. J. Fickert, *Franz Kafka. Life, Work and Criticism*, p8).

Kafka finally died in Vienna on 23 June 1924 and was buried in the family grave in the New Jewish Cemetery in Prague. For nearly all his life he had struggled with the schism of leading a respectable life and that of existing purely as a writer. He was unable to give up either but, symbolically, on his death bed, totally debilitated by his disease, '…he was incapable of doing anything but write' (K. J. Fickert, *Franz Kafka. Life, Work and Criticism*, p10).

* * *SUMMARY* * *

- Kafka spent practically the whole of his life living and working in the city of Prague.

- Kafka had continuous problems with his domineering father.

- Kafka constantly struggled with balancing his need to write with the expectation of leading the 'normal' middle-class life of holding down a decent job in an insurance company, getting married and settling down.

- He had a series of unfulfilled relationships with women, but they did provide him with the opportunity of writing hundreds of letters.

4 Social Background

A MAN OF HIS TIME

Kafka was very much a writer shaped by the social and historical world of his birthplace. He was born a Jew, but never fully practised his religion (although he took an intellectual interest in the faith, more towards the end of his life). He was born into a German-speaking family and educated in German schools, but was accepted into the Czech-speaking population being a Czech speaker with a Czech name. He led a socially acceptable life during the day, but was compelled to follow a literary and intellectual life at night.

FIN DE SIÈCLE

Europe, at the turn of the twentieth century, was an unstable and turbulent place. Kafka was producing his writing during and in the aftermath of World War I and, with stories like *In The Penal Colony*, would weave that influence into his words. 'As a writer, [Kafka's] affinities first lay with the decadent *fin-de-siècle*, then veered towards the violence associated with Expressionism, and finally reached a mode closer to the unadorned starkness typified by German *New Sobriety*.' (J. Adler, *Illustrated Lives: Franz Kafka*, p5.)

> **KEY TERM**
>
> *Fin se siècle*: Relating to the changes in morals and society pertaining to the end of the nineteenth and beginning of the twentieth centuries.

Europe was a changing place. The advance of technology, intellectual ideas and fashion made it an exciting place to be. Change was very much the flavour of the day. Prague was, according to the writer and artist André Breton, regarded as the 'secret capital of Europe', and '…a place where, politically, a new century was forged, and all the arts flourished' (J. Adler, *Illustrated Lives: Franz Kafka*, p15).

But change is unsettling with the loss of the old order and old habits for the new. As much as it was a celebratory time it was also an edgy time, especially politically.

The Czech nation was in the throes of nationalistic fervour against the **Hapsburg Empire** in the first half of the twentieth century. As World War I ended in defeat for the Germans, the German-Jews of Prague were caught in the middle with many who had supported the Germans swinging to support the Czech Emperor.

The **Bohemian** Germans no longer ran the bureaucracy of the country and as the new Republic of **Czechoslovakia** was formed in 1919, so the German language and the Germans fell victim. The German language was outlawed and many Germans and German-Jews were run out of their jobs and persecuted. Kafka, as a German-Jew, kept his job only because he was a Czech speaker and because he had never publicly declared allegiance to any one side.

THE PRAGUE CIRCLE

The 'Prague Circle' was the intellectual heart of the city. Although not an official group, the name incorporates the diverse thinkers of the time who involved themselves with contemporary issues from politics to culture to religion. Amid the shifting sands of the time, it afforded another weapon to be used:

KEY TERMS

Hapsburg Empire: German Princely family that ruled central Europe under the auspices of the Holy Roman Empire from 1440 to 1806. They provided rulers for central Europe including Austria, Spain and Bohemia. The line continued as the house of Hapsburg-Lorraine ruling Austria from 1806 to 1848 and Austria-Hungary from 1848 until 1918 when World War I brought an end to their rule.

Bohemian: Pertaining to Bohemia, a kingdom of central Europe. Independent from the ninth to the thirteenth centuries, it was ruled by the Hapsburgs up until 1918. It relates, mainly, to the Czech Republic and the Czech language.

Czechoslovakia: A republic formed, after the fall of the Hapsburg Empire, out of the Czechs in Bohemia and Moravia and the Slovaks in Slovakia. Occupied by the Germans in 1939 and then by the Soviet Union in 1945.

…culture was the weapon of choice on this battleground of nationality and ideology, as it was defined by the German-liberal ideologies. It was a game designed to give unique advantage to the Germans, which, however, did not prevent the Czechs from mastering the rules.

S. Spector, *Prague Territories*, p41

In amongst the political turmoil of the time, the continuing hostilities concerning the Jews and the advance of war, Prague maintained a strong intellectual heart. The Prague Circle, the group that Kafka was associated with, drank and discussed long into the evening. The group included writers such as Frank Werfel, Ergon Kisch, Hugo Bergmann, Otto Pick, Ernst Pollak and Max Brod.

The disproportionate literary production of the very small group of Kafka's generation was recognized early; in retrospect it calls the cultural historian's attention like a red flag marking the place where, if anywhere, a historical context provided rich ground for extraordinary texts.

S. Spector, *Prague Territories*, p5

These writers responded to the shifting political ground. Being in the heart of Europe they could not escape the turmoil of the time, but, as well as the larger picture, the Prague environment contained its own turmoil and change.

THE GHETTO

Kafka was born on the edge of the Prague Jewish **Ghetto**. The Ghetto had been established for over a thousand years and was a walled-off area of Prague filled with synagogues. It was also desperately overcrowded. The population of Prague Old Town was approximately 644 persons per hectare, whereas the Ghetto, in 1890, contained an average of 1,822 people per hectare.

KEY TERM

Ghetto: An area of a city that is segregated. It acts to isolate small populations.

With the passing of Emperor Joseph II's 'Toleration Edict' in 1782, many affluent Jews had moved out of the Ghetto. This caused the immigration into the area of criminals, people outside of society and prostitutes. It was also extremely unhygienic and disease-ridden. In 1890 the clean-up took place and the majority of the dark and twisting streets were demolished for 'sanitary' reasons. Another reason for the demolition came from the newly rich **bourgeoisie** who needed space for their new Art Nouveau buildings.

> ## KEY TERMS
>
> **Bourgeoisie:** The 'middle class'. In Marxist terms, the rich who oppress the workers.
>
> **Kosher:** That which accords to Jewish law. Food that is prepared in the correct dietary way in terms of Jewish law.

Kafka was witness to the demolition of the Ghetto and had memories of the old area with its shadowy alleys. He would describe the area as his 'prison cell – my fortress', a phrase that was as pertaining to the Jewish community as much as it was to him.

BEING JEWISH

The Ghetto was regularly attacked, hence the need for the wall. Even when the process of clearing the Ghetto was underway, the Jewish community erected a wire fence for protection. The mysterious, hidden Ghetto also fuelled wild, unfounded horror stories for the anti-Semitic element of Prague. There were stories of ritual murder carried out by the Jews, and rumours that the Jews needed Christian blood to make their unleavened bread. Kafka's grandfather had been a **Kosher** butcher so this story must have resounded in his imagination.

Although Kafka was not a regular practitioner of the faith, he still had his Bar-mitzvah and attended synagogue, but only sporadically. It was only later in life that Kafka took more than a glancing interest in the faith into which he was born.

KEEPING THE FAITH

It was a tricky time to be Jewish. Although, to be fair, it was also a tricky time to be German or Czech. Kafka upheld his interest in the Jewish faith in a more intellectual way rather than in a religious sense. It was thus possible to avoid the extremes of prejudice that were prevalent at the time.

His mature mind had always been **Talmudic**, full of exegesis and questioning of meaning; and he became increasingly drawn to the Zohar, the mystical readings of the **Torah**. This interest in turn was linked to his interest in language, and to his quest for words that would heal the split between what one felt and how that feeling could be expressed.

> **KEY TERMS**
>
> Talmudic (Talmud): The primary source of Jewish religious law.
>
> Torah: The scroll used in a synagogue service that contains Jewish teaching.

F. Karl, *Franz Kafka, Representative Man*,
p583

Kafka felt, as he did about most things, neither one thing nor another, neither Jewish nor non-Jewish, but he did find solace with the Yiddish actors of a travelling theatre troupe:

> Moreover, unlike most of Kafka's acquaintances, the Yiddish actors were not self-conscious about being Jews. In their company, Kafka could feel that he was no longer being labelled a Jew by the more or less hostile Gentile world; he was not compelled to accept other people's definitions of him; he was able to be a Jew and revel in it.

R. Robertson, *Kafka – Judaism, Politics and Literature*, p16

This friendship with the actors coupled with his interest in the intellectual and mystical elements of Jewish teachings, helped Kafka instinctively start to weave Jewish elements into his writing.

Even so, this expression appears as rather clandestine. Kafka played the elements of religion and politics close to his chest. It proved not only contrite (in Kafka's hands) but also to be valuable for self-preservation especially with the upheaval of World War I.

STUCK IN THE MIDDLE

The Czech Republic is, geographically, caught between East and West Europe. Prague, at the turn of the twentieth century, was a hot-pot mix of cultures, ideas and political and ideological schisms. There were many choices for the population to make. People took sides and, amongst all the uncertainty, it was a gamble as to which were the right choices:

On the one hand, [Kafka] felt drawn to the modernizing, western world, with its proliferating materialism and popular pleasures; whilst on the other, he was increasingly attracted to the archaic religion of his forebears, and a spirituality that he associated with the east.

J. Adler, *Illustrated Lives: Franz Kafka*, p5

The nature of the time was very factional. There was much persecution and battling between these sections that only added to the instability of the time. Yet Kafka avoided persecution despite being associated with the groups that attracted most attention – the Jews and the Germans.

Part of this revolved around his name. Kafka is a Czech name meaning 'jackdaw' and this afforded the family protection. Also, his parents brought him up as a Czech-speaker as well as a German one. In this way Kafka could integrate between the various communities of the city.

Kafka was often caught in the middle.

Also, his father had made a conscious decision to distance himself from the Jewish community. In this way he could attract a broader clientele to his shops, but it also provided a certain safety for his family from the anti-Semitic elements in the city.

Kafka mixed with the intellectuals from the university and with the 'Prague Circle' of writers and thinkers. Never being one to be up-front with his beliefs, Kafka could indulge in the influence of the group without being necessarily associated strongly with their particular standpoints.

Thus, Kafka acquired a vantage point where he could gain admittance to the various factions surrounding him and secure the ability to disappear between these communities and observe. Seen with hindsight, it appears that Kafka managed to manoeuvre around the cauldron that was Prague at that time. His life was guided by wise decisions by his parents and his own intellectual shyness. His natural quality of standing alone, combined with the climate of contemporary Prague, meant that Kafka:

> …belonged to no school. He stands alone – 'alone as Franz Kafka', he once said. His unique appeal, therefore, ultimately rests on the simplest paradox of all: all human beings are the same, but everyone is human in their own way.

J. Adler, *Illustrated Lives: Franz Kafka*, p8

* * * SUMMARY * * *

• At the turn of the twentieth century, Prague was a focal point between the East and West, old and new, and in the thick of the political upheaval that would bring about World War I.

• Kafka was Jewish, but he kept a distance from the faith.

• He was, by family culture, German but was brought up speaking Czech.

• He belonged to an intellectual group, the Prague Circle, but kept his distance. This way, he managed to side-step persecution.

Major Themes

DESCRIPTION OF A STRUGGLE

Kafka drew many of his themes from the intimate world around him: family, work and his personal struggle in his schizophrenic life of convention and art. Indeed, it could be said that his one main theme was struggle. Whether it is the struggle between father and son as in *The Judgement* or the struggle between an individual and authority as in *The Trial*, the effect remains the same – it is the conflict of the small against the overwhelming.

Within this struggle other themes are then explored. Through his writing, notions such as justice, guilt, and authority are examined. Kafka predominantly focuses on the individual as opposed to an ensemble of characters in his stories. His narratives follow these individuals on a complex and often absurd journey through an incomprehensible world whereby his themes are thus exposed.

JUSTICE

The universe of Kafka's writing translates to the reader as predominantly unfair. There seems to be little or no justice in his narratives. The world he creates is harsh and inflexible. In *The Trial*, for instance, the notion of justice is shown to be intransigent:

> '...the Court, once it has brought a charge against someone, is firmly convinced of the guilt of the accused and can be dislodged from that conviction only with the greatest difficulty.' 'The greatest difficulty?' cried the painter, flinging one hand in the air. 'Never in any case can the Court be dislodged from that conviction. If I were all the Judges in a row on one canvas and you were to plead your case before it, you would have more hope of success than before the actual Court.'

> F. Kafka, *The Trial*, p166

In this extract we see the fundamental twist that Kafka employs in his work – everyone is guilty until proven innocent, and, in the example of *The Trial*, that process of proving innocence is as good as impossible. The message declares that everyone is born guilty in someway.

Rarely is a fair trial seen in Kafka's work. In *The Judgement*, Georg is judged and condemned by the father, and in *The Metamorphosis* Gregor is judged by the family because of what he has wickedly and wilfully turned into. They judge Gregor not for who he is, but what he has, in their eyes, become:

> 'He must go,' cried Gregor's sister, 'that's the only solution, Father. You must try and get rid of the idea that this is Gregor. The fact that we've believed it for so long is the root of all our trouble.'

> F. Kafka (trans: W. and E. Muir), *The Penguin Complete Short Stories*,
> p134

The family has judged the situation believing that the creature is not Gregor at all and must be disposed of. The reader knows that it is still Gregor and is thus offered the opportunity to be sympathetic to the injustice of the situation. But what about the family? Where is the justice for them?

BEETLE, DUNG OR VERMIN?

There is some disagreement with translators as to the exact nature of Gregor's metamorphosis. It is usually taken to be an insect or, as is generally assumed, a dung beetle. This is not necessarily the case: 'The narrator…calls the creature *ein ungeheueres Ungeziefer*, of which the noun, *Ungeziefer*, is not very specific at all, something like English 'vermin', which some translators prefer to 'insect' or 'bug'. *Ungeheuer(es)* means 'monstrous.'' (R. H. Lawson, *Franz Kafka*, p30.)

By taking the broader view of Gregor's transformation, the themes become more disturbing. It would be understandable for the family to judge, somewhat harshly, what Gregor had become if he was *actually* a bug of some sort, but if you take the notion that Gregor had turned into something that his family and their society abhorred, for instance if the son of a staunch Conservative family had joined the Communist party, then the theme of judgement (and prejudice) becomes more pronounced.

Throughout Kafka's work, apparent unfairness is meted out regularly. The initial exile of Karl Rossmann in *Amerika* could be seen as unfair on *him*, but for his family it is the only solution to save themselves, as in *The Metamorphosis*. The treatment of K. by the authorities of the Castle in *The Castle* can be seen as unfair, but isn't it wise to keep the interloper at bay just in case?

It is easy to see just one side of the story with Kafka. The text presents the reader with only part of the argument. In doing this, by focusing mainly on the trials of the protagonist, a lopsided picture emerges. Kafka's heroes receive rough justice true enough, but the situations he creates tax both sides of the equation. Ultimately both sides are selfish in their desires which bring about the tensions in the narrative.

The text also presents unorthodox situations to systems of justice in his fiction. The justice is fair in terms of the system but, whether that justice is *actually* fair or not brings out, in the eyes of the reader, the emotional content of the work.

GUILT

In *The Trial*, Kafka takes the notion of guilt to a new height. With Kafka's work, guilt is more a product of paranoia than of accurate judgement. Joseph K. never finds out what he is being accused of but is, nonetheless, willing to accept his guilt. Logically, the notion of guilt can only exist if you know you have done something wrong, but, in Kafka's hands, guilt does not work that way. It can be inferred without reason. The characters are made to feel guilty without having done anything wrong, especially when consistently told of misdemeanours by an apparently uncaring outside world.

Guilt can turn the self against the self.

We can start to understand the guilt Gregor Samsa feels of not being able to go to work in *The Metamorphosis* when a representative of his work berates him:

> 'What's the matter with you? Here you are, barricading yourself in your room, giving only 'yes' and 'no' for answers, causing your parents a lot of unnecessary trouble and neglecting – I mention this only in passing – neglecting your business duties in an incredible fashion.'

> F. Kafka (trans: W. and E. Muir), *The Penguin Complete Short Stories*, p97

Guilt, again, is implied by Joseph K.'s uncle in *The Trial*.

> 'Joseph, my dear Joseph, think of yourself, think of your relatives, think of your good name. you have been a credit to us until now, you can't become a family disgrace. Your attitude,' he looked at K. with his head slightly cocked, 'doesn't please me at all, that isn't how an innocent man behaves if he's still in his senses.'

> F. Kafka, *The Trial*, p105

Rarely does a Kafka hero find total support for his situation. Inference of guilt is abundant even from those sympathetic to the **protagonist**. This increases the sense of isolation surrounding the central character. If the whole world believes you are not innocent

> **KEY TERM**
>
> Protagonist: The principle character in a play or novel.

it is easy to see yourself as guilty. In this way, Kafka's central characters become heroic in their self-belief and struggle.

AUTHORITY AND POWER

Father and Son

The tension between Kafka and his father is well documented in the diaries and letters. Kafka further explored this relationship in *Letter to Father* in 1919 opening the piece with:

> Dearest Father, You once asked me why I claim to be afraid of you. I did not know, as usual, what to answer, partly out of my fear for you and partly because the cause of this fear consists of too many details for me to put even halfway into words.

> F. Kafka, *Letter to Father*, p7

Kafka then goes on to try to explain this question in the following 65 pages and in the rest of his fictional work. Although a personal piece presented as fact, the theme of authority is explored in the writing:

> From your easychair you ruled the world. Your opinion was right, every other was mad, eccentric, *meshugge*, not normal. In fact, your self-confidence was so great that you did not have to be consistent at all and still never ceased to be right.

> F. Kafka, *Letter to Father*, p16

This exploration and commentary on authority is one of the cornerstones of Kafka's writing. It is difficult not to link Kafka's explorations of authority back to this father/son relationship. One of the most obvious 'fictional' stories Kafka wrote about this relationship with his father was *The Judgement* in 1913. The story has so many autobiographical elements – the bullying father, the son thinking of marriage to escape the father and the power games, all of which must have gone on in the Kafka household. Yet the ending is quite absurd – the son running off to throw himself off the bridge to oblivion. There is nothing in the story to warrant such an ending apart from the father's ultimate judgement:

> So now you know what else there was in your world besides yourself, till now you've known only about yourself! [sic] an innocent child, yes, that you were, truly, but still more truly have you been a devilish human being! – And therefore take note: I sentence you now to death by drowning!

> F. Kafka (trans: W. and E. Muir), *The Penguin Complete Short Stories*, p87

In Kafka's mind, the authority of his father's power remained absolute, and this notion of absolute power is a constant theme in his writing. Even in *In The Penal Colony*, where an old regime is coming to an end, there is the suggestion with the inscription on the headstone that the old authority is just lying dormant.

A bigger picture

After *The Judgement*, Kafka broadened his perspective to examine authority in all its different colours. *Amerika* takes the theme of the father/son battle and broadens it out to examine the control by a distant family and by acquaintances. Both *The Trial* and *The Castle* take this idea to represent greater, unseen powers that control and manipulate the individual.

By broadening these ideas the work of Kafka becomes universal, it becomes more than purely a personal exploration of the conflict revolving around the father. Those seemingly without power are standing in Kafka's shoes and those who appear to have the upper hand are standing in father Herman's shoes, regardless of the truth of the matter.

THREAT

Together with the obvious threats that are presented to his characters, Kafka creates threatening atmospheres in his work. In one of his early pieces, *Looking Out Absentmindedly*, even though there is a 'happy ending' of sorts and the setting is a spring day, which could be read as being positive, the feeling of foreboding is forever present:

> What will we do on these spring days that are so quickly approaching? Earlier today the sky was grey, but if you now go to the window, you are surprised and rest your cheek against its handle.

> Below, you see the light of the already setting sun on the face of a little girl, who looks around as she strolls, and at the same time you see upon it the shadow of a man who follows her at a quicker pace.

> Then the man has passed and the child's face is very bright.

> F. Kafka, *Meditations*, p43

The sense of menace and threat are very real and focused in part of one image – 'the shadow of a man who follows her at a quicker pace'. The threat of this image is compounded by the last line. The word 'bright' could refer to the physical brightness after the shadow has passed or it could refer to the relief the girl feels in the passing of the threat. Many of Kafka's main themes appear in this piece. Apparent here is the threat of an overpowering agent (the adult) over an innocent (the child). There is also the imposing situation over a powerless victim as with the shadow and the sense of trouble with the comment about the brightness of the girl's face after the shadow has passed. This implies and compounds the threat.

In another short piece, aphorism number 43 from *Reflections on Sin, Suffering, Hope, and the True Way*, the sense of threat is implied in a very concise way:

> The hunting dogs are still romping in the yard, but the prey will not escape them, however much it may be stampeding through the woods even now.

> F. Kafka, *The Blue Octavio Notebooks*, p90

Here the threat comes from the thought that the prey (the word immediately suggests victim), no matter how far they run, will not escape the hunting dogs. This notion of threat appears, obviously, in *The Trial*, but also in stories like *The Burrow*, written in 1923, where, no matter how defended the burrow is, the threat of another beast is constant and exhausting:

> And it is not only by external enemies that I am threatened. There are also enemies in the bowels of the earth. I have never seen them but legend tells of them and I firmly believe in them.
>
> F. Kafka (trans: W. and E. Muir), *The Penguin Complete Short Stories*, p326

The inference here is that there is threat from the inner world as well as the outer. Imagined threat is as dangerous as actual threat. Throughout Kafka's work, the mind of the hero is as dangerous to the situation as anything presented by outside forces.

FUTILITY

The way Kafka's heroes battle with their situations can, in terms of the narrative, appear as futile exercises. The feeling that the situation of the story will overwhelm the protagonist is always strong in his fiction. The story *The Country Doctor*, written in 1919, is an example of this.

The eponymous doctor has a patient he must visit urgently. He has to battle against severe winter weather and sort out a new horse because his own has died. The servant girl is being assaulted by the groom and the patient wants to die and then wants to live. The illness turns out not to be life-threatening and so the visit is unnecessary. The whole world seems to be conspiring against the doctor until he is overwhelmed with the futility of the situation: 'Betrayed! Betrayed! A false alarm on the night bell once answered – it cannot be made good, not ever.' (F. Kafka (trans: W. and E. Muir), *The Penguin Complete Short Stories*, p225.)

Kafka's protagonists find their actions futile, their plans thwarted at every turn. Everything Joseph K. does in *The Trial* has little or no effect other than make his case worse. K. in *The Castle* finds his attempts to gain entry to the Castle ineffective and Gregor's actions in *The Metamorphosis* are futile in his attempts to make the situation better.

The notion of futility is readily apparent in Kafka's short piece *Give it Up*. Here, the narrator is bluntly confronted with his situation by a policeman:

> [The policeman] smiled and said: 'You asking me the way?' 'Yes,' I said, 'since I can't find it myself.' 'Give it up! Give it up!' said he, and turned with a sudden jerk, like someone who wants to be alone with his laughter.
>
> F. Kafka (trans: W. and E. Muir), *The Penguin Complete Short Stories*, p456

In Kafka's fiction the hero cannot win. Every turn leads to more problems, uncertainty and frustration. In *The Bucket Rider*, the narrator goes to the coal dealer to beg for some coal for which he will pay at a later date. He is refused and this refusal seals his fate.

> 'You bad woman! I begged you for a shovelful of the worst coal and you would not give it to me.' And with that I ascend into the regions of the ice mountains and am lost forever.
>
> F. Kafka (trans: W. and E. Muir), *The Penguin Complete Short Stories*, p414

The sense of futility within Kafka's work is a strong, sometimes relentless, theme. The uncompromising, downbeat quality of the narratives is exhausting. Kafka's work is certainly not over-imbued with the feelgood factor. The work he puts his protagonists to is physically overpowering and spiritually testing. They are beaten but, ultimately, never defeated.

ANIMAL, MINERAL OR VEGETABLE

As a technique of storytelling and as a means of gaining a distance from, or a shifted perspective on, his themes, Kafka transformed many of his characters into or spoke from the point of view of animals or put them in animal settings.

Apart from the obvious change into a gigantic insect in *The Metamorphosis*, Kafka wrote from the point of view of a dog (*Investigations of a dog*), an ape (*Report to the Academy*), a mouse (*Josephine the Singer*) and a mole (*The Burrow*).

With *The Burrow*, Kafka filled the animal with human fears. The actions may not be recognisably anthropological but the emotions are. Kafka explores these feelings through the animal in its burrow – the fear of being found out, of noise, of constructing a safe world. This world is supposed to be secure but is ultimately vulnerable and the guilt of not constructing it properly haunts the animal.

Working in this way with animals, Kafka frees himself from the need to explore ideas or just to express feelings about the world around him. This expression sometimes topples beyond anguish and into cynicism, as with *A Little Fable*:

> 'Alas' said the mouse, 'the world is growing smaller every day. At the beginning it was so big that I was afraid, I kept running and running, and I was glad when at last I saw walls far away to the right and left, but these long walls have narrowed so quickly that I am in the last chamber already, and there in the corner stands the trap that I must run into.'
> 'You only need to change your direction,' said the cat, and ate it up.

> F. Kafka (trans: W. & E. Muir), *The Penguin Complete Short Stories*, p445

Once more, the themes of Kafka are contained in this small fable. The mouse is at a point of crisis and the cat has the power to assist and the ability to destroy the mouse. And if the cat doesn't get him, the trap will. This double bind highlights much of what Kafka investigated in his fiction.

ABSURDITY

It isn't just animals that Kafka endows with human emotions. In *The Bridge*, Kafka describes a bridge who is a person, or is it a person who is a bridge?

> I was stiff and cold, I was a bridge, I lay over a ravine. My toes on one side, my fingers clutching the other, I had clamped myself fast into the crumbling clay. The tails of my coat fluttered at my sides. Far below brawled the icy trout stream. No tourist strayed to this impassable height, the bridge was not traced on any map. So I lay and waited; I could only wait. Without falling, no bridge, once spanned, can cease to be a bridge.

And later in the same story when a traveller jumps on the bridge:

> Who was it? A child? A dream? A wayfarer? A suicide? A tempter? A destroyer? And I turned around so as to see him. A bridge to turn around!

> F. Kafka (trans: W. & E. Muir), *The Penguin Complete
> Short Stories*, p411

In this story Kafka acknowledges the absurdity of the situation and happily comments upon it and accommodates it easily in the narrative. It is quite acceptable in writing to imbue inanimate objects with human characteristics, but, what makes this absurd is the fact that the bridge recognises that maybe he shouldn't be a bridge. This revelation of knowledge suddenly blows the illusion and the whole piece becomes ridiculous.

Even a simple image in Kafka's hands can be unexpectedly absurd or surreal. The opening line of *Poseidon* illustrates this: 'Poseidon sat at his desk, going over the accounts. The administration of all the waters gave him endless work.' (F. Kafka (trans: T. & J. Stern) *The Penguin Complete Short Stories*, p434.) A simple image: the god of the sea being vexed by accounts. This gives Poseidon human weaknesses and he becomes comical in the process. At nearly every turn there is an absurd world in Kafka's fiction. The commentator on The Theatre of the Absurd, Martin Esslin comments that '[Kafka's] private fears had become flesh, had turned into the collective fear of nations; the vision of the world as absurd, arbitrary, and irrational had been proved a highly realistic assessment' (M. Esslin, *The Theatre of the Absurd*, p355).

The writer Eugene Ionesco, in an essay on Kafka, drew up the following definition of absurd writing: 'Absurd is that which is devoid of purpose...cut off from his religious, metaphysical, and transcendental roots, man is lost; all his actions become senseless, absurd, useless.' (*E. Ionesco*, 'Dans les armes de la ville', Cahiers de la Compagne, (Paris 1957), no. 20.) Certainly Kafka's work fits into this mould. Kafka creates absurd worlds to work symbolically, as with the image of the Statue of Liberty brandishing a sword in the opening of *Amerika*. Absurdity is also used to create tension or drama in the writing, for example, the conversation between the companions in *Description of a Struggle*:

> 'You've hurt yourself, eh? Well, it's icy and one must be careful – didn't you tell me so yourself? Does your head ache? No? Oh, the knee. H'm. That's bad.'

> But it didn't occur to him to help me up. I supported my head with my right hand, my elbow on a cobblestone, and said: 'Here we are together again.' And as my fear was beginning to return, I pressed both hands against his shinbone in order to push him away. 'Do go away,' I said.

> F. Kafka (trans: T. & J. Stern), *The Penguin Complete Short Stories*, p18

In this snippet there are certainly echoes of the interaction between Beckett's Vladimir and Estragon in his absurdist play *Waiting for Godot* (1952). Indeed practitioners of the Theatre of the Absurd in Paris of the 1940s and 1950s looked to the work of Kafka because of its absurdist content.

WHAT IS LIFE?

> The theme of Kafka's work is the theme of his life: the struggle of the
> self with itself to be itself.
>
>   H. Bloom, *Modern Critical Views: Franz Kafka*, p66

It is very tempting to mix Kafka's life and his work together. Kafka used
much of his own life and mind-set to inform his work. On first reading
Kafka's work it is very easy to get swept into the idea that a lot of it is
autobiographical. For instance, he worked in an insurance firm so it
would be logical to assume that *The Trial* makes direct reference to his
daytime working life.

There are intriguing connections between Kafka's fiction and his 'real'
life. If we look at some of the names he used for his characters, for
example, we can see some of the links. With *The Trial* he uses the name
Joseph K. Could the K refer to Kafka? In *The Castle* the name is rarefied
further to just K. Both novels examine themes that occupied Kafka,
specifically his battle between the conventional life and that of the
writer. In *The Metamorphosis* the name of the hero again makes
connections to Kafka: Samsa = Kafka. The vowels match up and the
consonants replicate in pattern in each name. In *The Judgement*, the
initials of the fictional fiancée share the same initials, F. B., with Kafka's
actual fiancée.

With his diaries, Kafka recorded events, mused on ideas and thoughts
and tried out pieces of fiction. Fact and fiction mix on the diary pages
and to draw a clear distinction between them is practically impossible.
In a way, Kafka encoded his own life into his fiction.

Kafka took his life and exaggerated it into fiction to explore his
concerns and themes. In effect, he moored his fiction in fact but gave
free rein to the interpretation of these facts in the conversion into
fiction. Kafka became his own fiction. We can look at his life and make
connections, but we must be aware the line between fact and fiction is

blurred and untrustworthy. Kafka took autobiography and '…by exaggerating, [he] created a grotesque and even comical-caricaturish distortions and so deformed perceptible reality, to make it more discernible.' (T. Anz, *Afterword, Letter to Father*, p76.)

In this way K. is and isn't Kafka. Ultimately, though, Kafka's work stands free from the author. If Kafka the man is removed from the equation, the texts still have a life of their own. The driving theme in Kafka's work was Kafka himself. This is fine for Kafka and those taking a biographical approach to the work but for the reader of the text and the text alone, it is merely a distraction.

THE STRUGGLE OF THE SELF

As an extension of applying himself in his work, another major theme in Kafka's writing was the more universal search for and understanding of the self. Like many writers, such as Beckett or Ionesco, Kafka was '…primarily concerned with trying to communicate his own sense of being, to tell the world what it feels like, what it means for him when he says 'I am' or 'I am alive' (M. Esslin, *The Theatre of the Absurd*, p158).

Kafka makes his characters struggle with who they are, with what they are supposed to be. If you look below the surface of his work, the search for identity or place in or outside society is strong. Kafka's characters battle with their place in the world. Was Joseph K. guilty or not guilty? Will his advocate or the artist give him the answers? Is the Castle a saviour or destroyer? What can be trusted and what is the true answer? Kafka explored this questioning in his writing: 'Kafka had to establish barriers to any compromise between fantasy and reality because his art depended on his uncertainty – on his depiction of uncertainty.' (F. Karl, *Franz Kafka, Representative Man*, p7.)

For Kafka his writing was a journey for the self and for balance.

✻ ✻ ✻ SUMMARY ✻ ✻ ✻

- Kafka's work revolved around struggle and attempts to understand the self.

- Kafka's home city of Prague offered a backdrop and a spirit to his writing.

- Kafka used and exaggerated autobiographical elements as a starting-off point to explore the themes in his writing.

- The friction between Kafka and his father was a constant theme throughout his writing. He then expanded this to be the struggle between the individual and authority.

- Kafka expressed his ideas as animals to further examine his explorations of guilt, powerlessness, authority and identity.

- There is a strong line of absurdity in his work, this absurdity exposing a deeper truth.

- Ultimately Kafka used his writing to explore ideas of the self and what it is to exist.

6 Major Works 1: The Novels

AMERIKA (ALSO KNOWN AS *THE MAN WHO DISAPPEARED*)

This was the first novel that Kafka wrote (between 1911 and 1914) and the last of the three novels he wrote to be published in 1927. *Amerika*, like the other novels, remains unfinished. Kafka had wanted to write a novel along the lines of Dickens' *David Copperfield* but, in a way, it has more of a feel of *Pinocchio* or even *Tom Jones* about it, in the sense of the 'innocent abroad'. *Amerika* is generally regarded as Kafka's most cheerful novel.

Amerika is the least visited of the three novels and the least 'Kafkaesque' even though it is still very much a Kafka novel. It still contains the battle between the two worlds of 'respectability' and 'freedom' with an individual searching for reasons or release. Even though the novel is seen as 'sunny', Michael Hofmann comments in his introduction to his translation of the novel that:

> There is an opposing reading of *The Man Who Disappeared*…that, far from being a jolly picaresque or Chaplinade, its events actually describe a pitiless descent through American society, towards a probable catastrophe every bit as grim and ineluctable as those in *The Trial* or *The Castle*.

> F. Kafka, *The Man Who Disappeared* (*Amerika*), px

The story opens with the hero, Karl Rossmann, arriving in America after being sent away by his parents because a maid had, allegedly, seduced him and had a baby by him. This first section originally appeared as a fragment called *The Stoker*.

Kafka's theme of guilt is established early on. Unlike Joseph K. in *The Trial*, we know from the outset which crime Rossmann has committed – that of impregnating the maid. In a way, Rossmann starts off as guilty and ends up innocent, whereas Joseph K. starts off as innocent and ends up guilty.

Familiar authority figures try to guide Rossmann, like his uncle who rescues him from the incident on the boat or the Head Porter who makes life a misery for the lift-boys in the hotel where Rossmann works. As there are characters representing the respectable world, so there are those who represent the other side of the tracks, namely the suspicious characters Robinson and Delamarche, who offer Karl refuge, but only use and abuse him.

In his essay *Amerika: Sinful Innocence*, Mark Spilka suggests that with this novel Kafka '…is preoccupied with sin rather than guilt, and with the possibilities of guilt and innocence which sinfulness involves'. He goes on to say: 'In America as in Europe, the child seems thwarted by familial and social pressures; he sins out of necessity, errs from youth and inexperience, and obeys degrading urges.' (M. Spilka, *'Dickens and Kafka: A Mutual Interpretation'*, (1963), H. Bloom (Ed), *Modern Critical Views: Franz Kafka*, (Chelsea House Publishers 1986), p61.) This is illustrated by the way Rossmann battles with the legitimate employment he finds and how he confronts his connections with the underbelly of society, finally escaping to the promise of the 'Nature' Theatre.

In the end, it is the 'Nature' Theatre of Oklahoma that acts as Karl's salvation:

> The Theatre of Oklahoma expresses for the last time the conflict between a child's dream of a world in which authority is not to be feared, in which faults are forgiven or overlooked, in which friends can stay together forever – and the melancholy knowledge that none of this can be.

> R. Spiers & B. Sandberg, *Franz Kafka*, p135

For Rossmann, this represents the perfect escape from the whirlwind of events that he has experienced. The 'Theatre' offers a haven for people of a like mind.

We can ascertain that Rossmann is on a conscious quest for a personal heaven but, with the last sentence, the perceived reality is typically bleak. Rossmann rides off into the sunset with this hope just about intact but still confronted by the coldness of a less optimistic reality. The last sentence sets the seal on the book and heralds what is to come with *The Trial* and *The Castle*. Karl escapes in a train over mountain rivers '…so close that the chill breath of them made their faces shudder' (F. Kafka, *The Man Who Disappeared (Amerika)*, p218).

THE TRIAL
The Trial was pieced together from the fragments that Kafka left. Some chapters were finished, others were incomplete and out of order. Max Brod pieced it together for publication in 1925.

This story is probably, together with *The Metamorphosis*, the best known of Kafka's writing. It defines the term 'Kafkaesque' and is the novel that certainly has most resonance in the world around us today. Written between 1914 and 1915, the basic premise is that the hero, Joseph K. '…without having done anything wrong…was arrested one fine morning' (F. Kafka, *The Trial*, p7). After this initial shock, the main struggle in the work is laid out:

> 'No,' said the man at the window, flinging the book down on the table and getting up. 'You can't go out, you are arrested.' 'So it seems,' said K. 'But what for?' he added. 'We are not authorized to tell you that.'

> F. Kafka, *The Trial*, p9

From that point onwards the action centres around Joseph K.'s desperate struggle to find out the means by which he can clear his name. The piece focuses on the process of unravelling an impossible legal system rather than on discovering what crime Joseph K. has committed. Indeed, the original German title was *Der Prozess (The Process)*, which fits the nature of the book better than the English translation *The Trial*, particularly as there is no legal trial in the piece.

Joseph K. spends the novel trying to find the truth of his situation and finding and rejecting support for his predicament. He begins with his landlady and his fellow lodger who both shy away from his plight. Then he turns to his advocate, Huld, who had been recommended by his uncle. This proves fruitless as Huld seems powerless in the constraints of the law and remains, fittingly, bedridden. Next, K. turns to the painter of official Court portraits, Titorelli, who seems to offer possible means of a solution, but in the end proves to be of as much use as Huld: 'Neither the path of living the conventional life [following the advocate]…nor the path of the Bohemian life [following the painter] leads to the solution of the riddle K. confronts: how guilt precedes the wrongful act and precludes atonement' (K. Fickert, *Franz Kafka, Life, Work & Criticism*, p21).

The last meaningful encounter K. has is with a priest who tells the parable *Before the Law*, a parable that reflects K.'s predicament – not being able to enter the law, or rather, not perceiving that he can enter the law. The door where the man from the country and the doorkeeper wait '…was both [meant] for the man *and* [meant] to be shut before he could enter it' (R. Spiers & B. Sandberg, *Franz Kafka*, p85).

Thus the torture of K's situation is amplified. The man from the country reflects K's situation. K. is seemingly impotent in entering the law, yet the solution is allegedly simple. He is free to enter the law but the system confuses the means to do so until it is too late. K. is held at bay by the law until his struggle has terminally entangled him in the unforgiving process.

Joseph K. cannot defend himself against unknown charges, his accusers are anonymous so he cannot cross examine them and the severity of the sentence is impossible to assess: 'Justice, by any normal definition, is simply not seen to be done.' (R. Spiers & B. Sandberg, *Franz Kafka*, p67.)

In the end K. is assassinated/executed on a piece of wasteland. The novel ends as it begins, with Joseph K. in a reclined posture. He starts off in bed, his head resting on the pillow, and ends on the wasteland with his head resting on a stone. This suggests a 'cradle to grave' notion in the novel. In this way, Joseph K.'s journey through the novel reflects a journey through life – birth, bewilderment, learning and inevitable demise.

In the end Joseph K. has been proven guilty by accusation only. He has become or has allowed himself to be guilty. He freely lets his two assassins do their job:

> With failing eyes K. could still see the two of them, cheek leaning against cheek, immediately before his face, watching the final act. 'Like a dog!' he said: it was as if he meant the shame of it to outlive him.

> F. Kafka (trans: W. & E. Muir), *The Trial*, p251

K. is losing sight of his situation. With his senses failing, he is letting go of his fight. It is as if he is finally accepting his situation with the 'shame', in this context, appearing to be the final admission of guilt.

THE CASTLE

The Castle, written in 1922, again was an unfinished novel pieced together by Brod. The original publication of 1926 finishes in the midst of chapter 18; later editions after 1951 include the whole of chapter 18 and chapters 19 and 20. Even so, the novel ends abruptly. In one of its earliest notes, the title of *Temptation in the Village* was suggested by Kafka in his diary.

The name of hero of the story is here pared down to just the letter K. Apparently, the book was started in the first person. 'K' then replaced the first person 'I'. The rest of the book was then written in the third person. By doing this, the first-person narrator becomes as much an outsider to the story as K. is the outsider to the village. This echoes *The Trial* in the sense that both K.'s find themselves placed at the edge of their respective dramas. 'Gradually the ambiguities surrounding K.'s uncertain position in the village make it analogous to the situation of the Jew in an anti-Semitic environment and, more resonantly, to the human condition' (R. Hayman, *K: A Biography of Franz Kafka*, p274).

Like *The Trial*, the novel is effective in creating an overall atmosphere. Again, the story is episodic. The effect is more akin to watching a lab rat in a behavioural experiment. K. has been summoned to the Castle to work as a surveyor, but on his arrival at the village at the foot of the Castle hill it is not clear what exactly he has to do or if he is actually needed. All through the novel it is never made clear if he is actually needed by the 'Castle'. He arrives at the Castle desperate to do his work, but never achieves it. He seems to be thwarted, not just by the Castle but by the village as well.

In the meantime, K. gets enmeshed in the lives of the villagers. He strikes up relationships – most notably with women – and finds a job as a school janitor. All the while he still focuses on getting the acceptance of the Castle. Again, the notion of the individual's struggle between two worlds is evoked as K. is seduced by the Castle and village and his emotional connections with it.

A Towering Symbol
The novel has spiritual overtones, as well as depicting a bureaucracy gone mad. The Castle is a huge symbol in the novel, representing a greater power: mysterious and distant yet essential in the lives of the characters. The symbolism of the Castle itself can be viewed in various ways, as representing:

* the unbreakable authority of the father or God;

* the fortress of the self and self-knowledge;

* the fortress of spiritual enlightenment;

* the search for an emotional and sexual union, the Castle representing the unobtainable.

The Castle can also be seen as the idea of a nationalistic identity, existing purely as an abstract thought: 'The Castle hill was hidden, veiled in mist and darkness, nor was there even a glimmer of light to show that the castle was there.' (F. Kafka, *The Castle*, p9.)

By shrouding the Castle in mist, it becomes abstract. The presence, however, is felt even when there is no visual presence. It is as if the Castle is being hidden in a veil of secrets and whispers. Nothing is stated for sure – the interpretation is left open. Whatever the symbolism of the Castle, it stands as a journeys end: '...*The Castle* is a terminus of soul and mind, a *non plus ultra* of existence' (E. Heller, 'Kafka' (1974), in H. Bloom (Ed), *Modern Critical Views: Franz Kafka*, p136.)

Heller sees *The Castle* as *the* final point. Acceptance into the Castle is the last action. It can be seen in terms of gaining entry in to heaven, Valhalla or oblivion. Whatever the reading, the Castle looms over the landscape exuding the feel that this is the end of the world – in all senses of the word.

That said, the novel itself is a journey without end. The last line is inconclusive:

> K. was already in the hall and Gerstäker was clutching at his sleeve again, when the landlady shouted after him: 'I am getting a new dress tomorrow, perhaps I shall send for you.'

> F. Kafka, *The Castle*, p298

By referring to 'tomorrow', K.'s journey, as with Joseph K. in *The Trial*, appears infinite. It leaves K. in the position that his journey has potentially ground to a halt, repeating itself rather than ending. He is caught in stasis with acceptance by the Castle as the only way out.

Kafka had suggested an ending where K. is on his death-bed and finally gets acceptance from the Castle. This, for whatever reason, was rejected. As the ending stands, Ronald Spiers and Beatrice Sandberg suggest that:

...K's unintended but proper destination is a place where the essential incompleteness of human life, which in his case is a life driven by a will obsessed with empty images of power and authority, is revealed, but not recognized.

R. Spiers & B. Sandberg, *Franz Kafka*, p135

By this, K.'s journey is true. There is no overt deception in the reason why he is there, but the resolution will never occur. In a very downbeat way, the only solution seems to be death itself.

The Castle was written towards the end of Kafka's life. Another view of the novel relates its vision with Kafka's declining health: 'Indeed, the very physical presence of the castle looming on the hill overlooking the inn and the village suggests the isolation of the sanatorium.' (S. Gilman, *Franz Kafka, The Jewish Patient*, p235.)

The suggestion here is that the scenario reflects the situation of Kafka's hospitalization.

In spite of having the atmosphere of a middle European village, the novel is self-contained within its own landscape. It focuses on its own universal themes. Max Brod highlights this when he says that '...Kafka's *Castle*, for all the individuality of the character it describes, is a book in which everyone recognizes his own experiences' (M. Brod, *Franz Kafka*, p186).

THE NOVELS AS A TRILOGY

Each novel is independent of each other with their own concerns and conceits. Yet, taken as a whole, they can also be seen as a coherent trilogy. Looking at the three novels in the order that they were written – *Amerika*, *The Trial* and *The Castle* – a pattern can be traced through the journeys of the protagonists, (or protagonist – it seems that it is the same character journeying through the three novels). *Amerika* can be seen as representing the journey from birth through childhood, *The Trial* as a journey through 'adulthood' and *The Castle* as a spiritual finality.

The three novels can be seen as a single journey.

In *Amerika* the hero finds he is born into the bewildering newness of life in 'America'. The journey leads him in search of the self in terms of a promised-land. At the end he heads off with optimism but riding into a chill wind. In *The Trial* the notion of searching is developed to explore the self in terms of the struggle towards freedom from guilt. In the end the guilt 'kills' Joseph K, but the outcome could be seen as a release from the bureaucracy of an accusing world. In *The Castle*, K. is involved with the search, or quest, for the self in terms of a final, total acceptance. The acceptance by who or what is left open for interpretation.

This journey through the three books encompasses a journey to 'salvation' from the physical world to the spiritual or the essence of humanity. Each step, or novel, is rarefied from a real world to a spiritual one.

If the protagonists are seen as one entity, this singularity can be seen in the way their names are pared down from Karl Rossmann to Joseph K. to just K. The landscapes become more mysterious as the novels progress. The striking opening image of the sun-drenched Statue of Liberty in *Amerika* turns into the derelict feel of *The Trial* which, in turn, gives way to the overwhelmingly dark and intangible landscape of *The Castle*.

There is also a developmental link between the reasons why the protagonists are in their particular situations. All three are cast out of an innocent world. Rossmann has been cast into the New World of *Amerika* because of a sexual liaison with a servant. Joseph K. is cast into a 'New World' because of a legal 'loss of innocence'. K. is cast into an uncertain 'New World' because the Castle won't accept his 'innocent' reason for being there.

✹ ✹ ✹ SUMMARY ✹ ✹ ✹

● The novels were never fully finished pieces of work. They are fragmentary and episodically constructed.

● All three concern an individual on a journey or quest for a truth.

● *The Trial* is a perfect illustration of the term 'Kafkaesque'.

● The three novels can be seen as both independent from each other, each having their own concerns, and as a progressive trilogy.

---

7 Major Works 2: The Shorter Fiction

THE JUDGEMENT

At ten o'clock in the evening of 22 September 1912 the twenty-nine-year-old Franz Kafka sat down to begin his story 'Das Urteil' (*The Judgement*). When he finished it at six in the morning, his legs so stiff he could hardly pull them from under his desk, he knew he had used his talent as never before.

R. Hayman, *K: A Biography of Franz Kafka*, p1

The Judgement, published in 1913, was Kafka's first significant story and contains all the elements of his distinctive storytelling. It was the first outing for the continuous struggle in his life and writing between the higher authority and the guilty individual.

The narrative is simple to the point of non-existence. Georg and his father have shared a flat together since Georg's mother died two years previously. Apart from business and meetings over lunch neither man sees much of each other. Georg has just written a letter telling of his recent engagement to a friend in St. Petersburg and goes to tell his father about this. His father doesn't believe that Georg has a friend in Russia and the discussion escalates into the father berating the son until he finally bellows:

So now you know what else there was in the world besides yourself, till now you've known only about yourself! An innocent child, yes, that you were, truly, but still more truly have you been a devilish human being! – And therefore take note: I sentence you now to death by drowning!

F. Kafka (trans: W. and E. Muir), *The Penguin Complete Short Stories*, p87

At which point Georg takes to his heels and runs off to throw himself from the local bridge.

This is an absurdist story that caricatures the relationship between father and son and the struggle for dominance and power – the father fights back from a position of submission by an eruption of power which ultimately destroys his son. Also, the father is outraged that his son is *writing* to his friend – another parallel with the real life of Kafka and his continual hang-up of balancing his writing with his other life. Alwin L. Baum, in his essay *Parable as Paradox in Kafka's Stories*, says:

> As with Kafka, Georg's fiancée and his father come between him and the friend whose role is perhaps best associated with the estranged alter-ego of the writer. Like his father, Georg's friend is victim of his neglect, and has even 'turned yellow enough to be thrown away.'

A. L. Baum, *Parable as Paradox in Kafka's Stories* (1976)
H. Bloom (Ed), *Modern Critical Views: Franz Kafka*, p163

Another point in this story is revealed by his father's tirade. By the father's extreme outburst and sudden command of the situation he becomes the puppet master: 'But your friend hasn't been betrayed after all!' cried his father, emphasising the point with stabs of his forefinger. 'I've been representing him here on the spot.' (F. Kafka (trans: W. and E. Muir), *The Penguin Complete Short Stories*, p87.)

By this, the father demonstrates that he has influence or control over *every* aspect of Georg's life.

Ultimately, this is a story of power and submission. Georg has held 'power' over the father. The father is initially seen as enfeebled and cared for by the son. Then there is the grotesque switch of control and it is the son who is suddenly enfeebled.

Georg acquiesces in his father's coarse annihilation of Frieda Brandenfeld. Georg surrenders her, as he surrenders his friendship with the friend in Petersburg. All he can do is mock the father, call him a comedian, a designation the father gladly and not illogically accepts. Surrender here, surrender there – does the reader doubt that Georg will also surrender his own life and his writing (the unsent letter still in his pocket)?

R. H. Lawson, *Franz Kafka*, p24

In conclusion, the apparent power the son has over his father becomes illusory. The power of the father figure is absolute, even when it appears weak. For Georg, the ending is not only an extreme adherence to the father's condemnation but also the realization of how his belief in controlling his own life has been somewhat of a sham.

THE METAMORPHOSIS

Apart from *The Trial*, *The Metamorphosis* is perhaps the most striking piece of writing that Kafka produced. It was written at the end of 1912 and published in October 1915. The basic premise is that Gregor Samsa, a travelling salesman living at home and supporting his family with his wage, turns into a gigantic insect. But his change is only physical, his psychological self remains human. The bulk of the story revolves around how his relationship with his family deteriorates and how, rather than descending into self-pity, Gregor's only drive is to make the unfortunate situation better.

This is a defining 'Kafka' story. There is very little narrative: a man turns into an insect and the family isn't happy. He dies and the family are happy. But, there are layers upon layers of meaning contained in the description of the crisis the characters face, hide from and confront.

Does Gregor represent the state of mind of the family unit? Is the change of physical form symbolic of Gregor's feeling of isolation from the family unit? Is this, again, a representation of a father/son power struggle with the bombastic father ultimately responsible for Gregor's decay?

Transformations were real events.

One of the strongest elements, and an example of how Kafka could make the most extraordinary situation seem normal, is the way he deals, or doesn't deal, with the change itself. The characters react to the state Gregor is in, believing that he is ill rather than changed, but never is the question raised as to why or how the change has taken place. It is as if the change from human to insect form is an everyday, if inconvenient, occurrence.

The change, though, is real enough. 'What has happened to me, he thought? This was no dream.' (F. Kafka (trans: W. and E. Muir), *The Penguin Complete Short Stories*, p89.) The situation is actually happening. The nightmare has become a physical reality and Gregor cannot wake up from it. What has happened to Gregor can be read as the result of his situation:

> ...it is a valid critical insight that Gregor, as a loathsome insect, has become that which he was made to feel by his family, especially his father; but also by his employer, by his life as a travelling salesman, by...his society, that is, by exploitive, rapacious, dehumanizing, capitalist industrial society.

R. H. Lawson, Franz Kafka, p29

Gregor has turned into the being that he believed himself to be.

We can take the notion of Gregor as a psychological symbol for the family as a group, as David Eggenschwiller suggests in his essay '*The Metamorphosis*':

> Gregor now becomes, in a psychological sense, the main symbol of what they experience in economic, social, and domestic relationships, they do not deal with him directly until their crisis, until they must confront all of their problems as represented by him. Until then they turn their attention outward, enduring the symptoms of their essential problems, not facing and acting on the causes.

D. Eggenschwiller, 'The Metamorphosis' (1979), H. Bloom (Ed.),
Modern Critical Views: Franz Kafka, p208

We can see that Gregor is, in one view, an invention of the family's mind-set. Both the family and Gregor reflect each other. For the family, Gregor represents social shame and for Gregor, the family reflects the creature he has become.

Thus when he dies, or the family solves their problem, the remaining family flourish as a coherent unit. At that point his sister suddenly blossoms with youth and beauty. New life has replaced old. Also, the socially unacceptable Gregor has stopped plaguing the parents and cursing them in society, being replaced by a more than acceptable daughter.

Whatever reading is taken of *The Metamorphosis*, it still remains a powerful piece of literature. It is both horrific and pathetic, realistic and absurdist. It is a deceptively simple story that haunts the mind for a very long time.

It is the most startling statement any writer has made in shorter form, and it is doubly compelling because it refuses interpretation. One can see it only as 'possibilities' and 'potentialities'. And even the effort to link the novella to Kafka's own life uncovers several discrepancies. The most satisfactory yield comes from letting the novella do its own work, without intrusion.

F. Karl, *Franz Kafka: Representative Man*, p463

IN THE PENAL COLONY

'It's a remarkable piece of apparatus,' said the officer to the explorer and surveyed with a certain air of admiration the apparatus which was after all quite familiar to him.

F. Kafka (trans: W. and E. Muir), *The Penguin Complete Short Stories*, p140

Thus opens *In The Penal Colony*, written in 1914 and published in 1919. As was Kafka's wont, there is little if no story. He invokes the atmosphere of the situation and captures, in detail, a telling moment in the lives of the characters.

Once again there is a death, lovingly described, but this time it revolves around the authoritarian officer and the demise of a defunct regime.

And here, almost against his will, he had to look at the face of the corpse. It was as it had been in life; no sign was visible of the promised redemption; what the others had found in the machine the officer had not found; the lips were firmly pressed together, the eyes were open, with the same expression as in life, the look was calm and convinced, through the forehead went the point of the great iron spike.

F. Kafka (trans: W. and E. Muir), *The Penguin Complete Short Stories*, p166

The officer had been the last in command of the Penal Colony being visited by the humanitarian explorer. The machine of execution being demonstrated to the explorer was the pride of the regime's authority – through execution comes enlightenment and acceptance of guilt. As if in demonstration of this ideology and recognition of the end of the line for everything the officer believes in, he submits himself to the punishment over which he presided.

Although there seems to be an initial reversal of Kafka's themes – the immovable higher authority in this case is crumbling – the work continues to explore authoritarian relationships.

> Kafka continues in *In The Penal Colony* to employ the themes and figures firmly established in his earlier work: the Old Commandant is basically a variation of the stern father; the dutiful son who sacrifices himself appears in the form of the officer. The traveller can be seen as a variant of another Kafka alter ego – the rebel, the opponent of the father, who observes the world of the older generation and rejects it.
>
> K. Fickert, *Franz Kafka. Life, Work and Criticism*, p22

Thus the characters in *In The Penal Colony* still conform to the Kafka blueprint. By presenting them in a different light, another perspective of the relationship of power and its use and abuse can be examined.

Within the story, though, there are different layers of comprehension. One of the more prominent metaphors is in the connection between the machine of execution and ritual Jewish slaughter or **shehitah**.

> **KEY TERM**
>
> Shehitah: Jewish ritual slaughter to produce Kosher meat.

> The attack on shehitah as cruel and heartless compared to modern forms of ritual slaughter is echoed in Kafka's later story *In The Penal Colony*…However, the machine combines the modern forms of slaughter advocated by the opponents of shehitah, clearly condemning them, with the ritualism associated with shehitah.
>
> S. Gilman, *Franz Kafka, The Jewish Patient*, p150

The machine can also be taken in Christian terms. Rose Lawson sees the story as symbolic of the events told in the Bible: '…*In The Penal Colony* may be read as a thought-provoking fragmentary parallel to the crucifixion of Christ, in which the execution machine serves as an analogue of the cross.' (R. H. Lawson, *Franz Kafka*, p92.)

The execution, according to the officer, brings about transfiguration in the condemned as they are tattooed with their sentence. Like the Christian story, the execution is about forgiveness and redemption. Thus the condemned are forced to accept their sin and are allowed into heaven.

Even though the old regime is seen to be on the verge of extinction, there is a warning enscribed on the Old Commandant's headstone: 'There is a prophecy that after a certain number of years the Commandant will rise again and lead his adherents from this house to recover the colony.' (F. Kafka (trans: W. and E. Muir), *The Penguin Complete Short Stories*, p167.)

Here is the potential danger of a resurgence of the old regime. The old powers could return, just as the power of the father returned in *The Judgement*.

There are also sexual, sadistic and masochistic parallels in the story. The machine itself seems to be a mix of sexual descriptions – the condemned lie on the quivering bed, the needles penetrate the skin, and the harrow is described as limp and then rigid. 'The Harrow appears to do its work with uniform regularity. As it quivers, its points pierce the skin of the body with itself quivering from the vibrations of the bed.' (F. Kafka (trans: W. and E. Muir), *The Penguin Complete Short Stories*, p147.) The erotic suggestion is compounded by the fact that the condemned man or woman is strapped naked to the bed.

There is a strong link between pleasure and pain and the text explores this. The relish in the officer's description of the machine and the declaration that the process of execution will bring absolution presents the promise of pleasure. It also raises the question of masochism and sadism reflecting the fascination for torture. The explorer is both fascinated and repelled by the machine and its purpose.

A HUNGER ARTIST

A *Hunger Artist*, written and published in 1922, was one of the last pieces of writing that Kafka worked on. This time the bizarre heart of the story concerns a side-show attraction – the 'hunger artist' – a man on view to the public who starves himself to the point of death. Initially he was a great attraction, with people coming to admire his skills. Every fortieth day of the fast, the Impresario would feed him at a celebratory feast and the routine would start all over again. But, eventually the crowds lost interest and he got overlooked. Then an overseer spotted the seemingly unused cage and questioned the man about his fasting:

> 'I always wanted you to admire my fasting,' said the hunger artist. 'We do admire it,' said the overseer, affably. 'But you shouldn't admire it,' said the hunger artist. 'Well then we don't admire it,' said the overseer, 'but why shouldn't we admire it?' 'Because I have to fast, I can't help it,' said the hunger artist. 'What a fellow you are,' said the overseer, 'and why can't you help it?' 'Because,' said the hunger artist, lifting his head a little and speaking, with his lips pursed, as if for a kiss, right into the overseer's ear, so that no syllable might be lost, 'because I couldn't find the food I liked. If I had found it, believe me, I should have made no fuss and stuffed myself like you or anyone else.'

> F. Kafka (trans: W. & E. Muir), *The Penguin Complete Short Stories*, p277

With this the hunger artist dies and, as in *The Metamorphosis*, new, stronger life replaces him, this time in the shape of a Black Panther.

The tone of the story implies that anything that is done through need should not be regarded as worthy. The side-show 'freak' is lauded because of his actions. The thrust of the story exposes this notion. Why should the public be interested in a man who is only doing what he does naturally? Taken further, this notion can be applied to anyone who stands outside of what society would regard as 'normal' – the artist or writer for instance.

There are many absurd elements to this story. Putting on a public display of the act of starvation is a grotesque notion, yet there was, initially, an audience for it. The artist himself is not fasting out of choice and is not resisting temptation, even though there is an enticing parallel to Christ resisting temptation in the wilderness for 40 days. The artist is finally replaced by a more alluring side-show. Despite the signals, the story is '…show business. That is to say, the practising of welcome deception, for profit' (R. H. Lawson, *Franz Kafka*, p92).

The artist, despite his state, is complicit with the spectacle he has become and with how the showman wishes to present him to the crowds. The artist does not rage against his circumstances and, unlike many of Kafka's protagonists, he co-operates with the situation until he is merely overlooked. The world kills him by disinterest rather than by interacting with him. He, in reply, goes quietly.

This story, like *The Judgement*, has another, more personal drive. With *The Hunger Artist*, it is as if Kafka is having a last, absurd rage against himself, his situation and his world:

> …obviously the story is developed out of self-criticism, while images of caging, chains and imprisonment were recurrent in his conversation. The 'I' is nothing…but a cage from the past, its bars intertwined with incessant dreams of the future.

> R. Hayman, *K: A Biography of Kafka*, p273

Kafka may also be taking a side-swipe at his friend Max Brod in the portrayal of the impresario who talks up the genius of the hunger artist.

It would be too obvious to link the metaphor of the food to Kafka's writing. It is possibly better – considering that he knew he was dying – to look at the food as a metaphor for the life he had wanted to live; the options he had tried that he never fully liked.

In the end autobiography and writing come together. It is ironic to think that Kafka was working on final drafts of this story as he was suffering from tuberculosis. The tuberculosis was swelling up his larynx so that he was unable to eat and thus he, like the artist, was starving to death.

* * * *SUMMARY* * * *

● Kafka's work was constantly linked in some way to his life. Even so, the stories are exaggerations of Kafka's biography and thus free themselves from Kafka to explore ideas of self and power.

● Kafka's work is open to interpretation from a plethora of differing views, from religion to sexuality.

● Although personal in nature, Kafka's work reaches out to reflect a universal search for meaning in the world.

● His stories work as concentrated moments, examining situations rather than working within a framework of narrative driven stories.

● The layers of meaning in his work are a natural part of Kafka's writing rather than being contrived constructs imposed on it.

Contemporary Critical Approaches

EARLY REVIEWS

The work of Kafka failed to take the world by storm in the first few years it existed in the market place. Kafka was never a self-promoter and took a dissatisfied view of his work, calling for its destruction upon his death. Even so, reviews of his first collection of writings, *Meditations*, published in 1913, were quite positive.

Reviews ranged from the ambiguous:

> Kafka's little meditations form something previously unknown in German Literature; I know no model.

> Hans Kohn in *Selbstwehr*, 20 December 1912

… to the curious:

> Stylistically unbelievably mature, with the facility of the French masters, rhythmic as the lamentations of lonely young women…

> Otto Pick in *Bohemia*, 30 January 1913

… to the cheerleading:

> A strangely lyrical prose, without punch lines, less cleverly witty than Peter Altenberg. A remarkably great, remarkably refined book by an ingeniously sensitive writer!

> Albert Ehrenstein in *Berliner Tagblatt*, 16 April 1913

In spite of these encouraging reviews, it took a long time for Kafka to reach his now mythical stature in the Western literary canon. Much of this credit is due to the effort that his friend Max Brod put into piecing Kafka's fragments together to make a coherent whole and getting the work published posthumously.

MAX BROD

Brod was the major champion of Kafka's work, especially after Kafka's death. Not only did he salvage Kafka's writing from the author's own destructive wishes but he edited the work, piecing it together from a mish-mash of scraps and fragments, following instructions from his memory of what his friend had said to him.

Brod had writing aspirations of his own, but put a lot of energy into promoting Kafka and making sure that his work did not sink without trace. The world may never have heard of Kafka if it wasn't for the efforts of Brod. The irony is that Brod then had to live in Kafka's shadow. He is better known as Kafka's editor rather than as a novelist and literary figure in his own right. Kafka and Brod – the two names were and always will be linked.

SWAMPED BY HISTORY

Condemned at home

Kafka's work had an initial rough ride when released into the public domain. Czech Nationalism was all-engulfing when the country broke free from the Hapsburg Empire in 1919. Unfortunately Kafka wrote in German. Because of this, and because he painted such a dark and foreboding assumed picture of Prague in his stories, his work was very difficult, if not impossible, to get hold of. In the decade after Kafka's death, none of his books were available in his native land. Even Czech translations were rare.

The Nazis walk on by

If this seemed a bit harsh, then worse was to follow. The Nazi Party was gaining popularity and momentum in the 1930s. In 1939, Germany occupied Czechoslovakia. As the Nazi Party and World War II swept across Europe, any of Kafka's work that had not been collected by Brod was destroyed by the Germans. Being a Jewish writer his books were burned and outlawed.

Uncle Joe

Then, in 1948, the Soviets took control of Czechoslovakia and Kafka was once again banned. This time, as the Marxist critic Georg Lukács said, for being a 'decadent modernist'.

However, Kafka's work struck resonance with those opposed to the Soviet Regime. At a time when the **KGB** and its informers were active, *The Trial*, for instance, became incredibly prophetic and it was read, illegally, as a *realistic* representation of life under Stalin. Indeed,

> **KEY TERM**
>
> KGB: *Komitet Gosudarstvennoi Bezopasnosti* – the Soviet secret police.

much of Kafka's work foretold many of the conflicts middle Europe would experience – persecution, fear, oppression and tyranny. The Stalinist regime revelled in show trials, publicly accusing ex-Communist leaders of crimes they had not committed. Joseph K. had stepped from fiction into fact.

Kafka's work was seen as subversive.

In one of his most prophetic pieces, *The Fist in the Coat of Arms*, Kafka foretold:

> All the legends and songs which have originated in this city are filled with the longing for the prophesized day on which the city will be smashed to pieces by five successive blows from a gigantic fist.

H. Salfellner, *Franz Kafka and Prague*, p189

Prague, like most of Middle and Eastern Europe, was being smashed by the fists of war. For many experiencing this period of history, Kafka's work represented their situation.

Other voices

Instead of running the gauntlet of critical review, Kafka's work became linked with fighting against the 'regime' whether it was Nationalism, Imperialism or Communism. In that way Kafka's work became almost untouchable to critics except for those that felt threatened by it. Even so, critic Edmund Wilson offered a dissident view:

> I find it impossible to take [Kafka] seriously as a major writer and have never ceased to be amazed at the number of people who can…To compare Kafka…with Joyce and Proust and even with Dante…is obviously quite absurd…I do not see how one can possibly take him for either a great artist or moral guide.

E. Wilson, *A Dissenting Opinion on Kafka*, (Internet source Leni's Franz Kafka Page 2001)

That being said, others, such as the writer **Vladimir Nabokov** regarded Kafka as 'the greatest German writer of our time'.

KEY TERM

Vladimir Nobokov: 1899–1977. Russian-born, American writer. Author of *Lolita*.

All the while, Kafka's work was slowly making its presence felt with those whose business was literature. His work was available but little known in the West. In his introduction to the 1930 English translation of *The Castle*, Edwin Muir says:

'Franz Kafka's name, so far as I can discover, is almost unknown to English readers. As he is considered by several of the best German critics to have been perhaps the most interesting writer of his generation, and as he is in some ways a strange and disconcerting genius, it has been suggested that a short introductory note should be provided...'

F. Kafka, *The Castle*, p7

So, Kafka arrived in English translation as an 'interesting' writer who needed a bit of explanation. But he had already picked up the tag of 'genius'. Most reviews of this strange writer were favourable, but, in a way, his work wasn't really for the literary erudite. Kafka's writing came into its own due to the circumstances of war, occupation and through the fascination of those who struggled to keep their identity against an overwhelming authority.

HERALD OF THE 'PRAGUE SPRING'

In 1963, a 'Kafka Congress' was held near Prague which made a start to establishing his reputation to the level of fame we see today. A celebration of the work of Kafka formed part of the Writers' Union Congress at Liblice as a celebration of the 80th anniversary of his birth. Kafka was finally brought in from the cold. He was being re-invented for Czech communists as a champion raging against the rise of an Imperialistic Western world.

More than that, for many, in retrospect, this praise of Kafka was regarded as the beginning of the 'Prague Spring', the brief rebellion against the Soviet Occupation which was eventually crushed in 1968. Once the Soviets had regained their domination, Kafka's work was again outlawed.

By then, however, Kafka's reputation was intact and was being embraced by a new generation of readers. His grave in Prague became a major attraction for visitors. The genie was out of the bottle and Kafka was elevated, seemingly directly, from the little-known German-speaking writer from Prague to the phenomenon he is seen as today.

As his relationship with his father helped form Kafka the writer, so the traumas of Europe helped make his writing one of the cornerstones of twentieth-century literature.

* * * *SUMMARY* * * *

● In his day, Kafka received favourable but not spectacular reviews.

● The events of European history helped establish Kafka's writing as a powerful expression of the fight against oppressive regimes.

● For many years the work of Kafka was outlawed by the various controlling powers of the Republic of Czechoslovakia. He was banned by the Nationalistic Czechs, by the Nazis and by the Soviet Union.

● Under the Soviet regime, Kafka's work was read as realistic rather than as parable or allegory.

Modern Critical Approaches

'AS FRANZ KAFKA AWOKE ONE MORNING FROM UNEASY DREAMS HE FOUND HIMSELF TRANSFORMED IN HIS BED INTO A GIGANTIC WRITER'.

One of the reasons that a piece of writing becomes a 'classic' is when it can be interpreted in various ways. Kafka's work has been poured over by many theorists and critics who apply their own interpretations of the significance of his writings. His texts are thus opened up to multiple interpretations. Susan Sontag comments:

> The work of Kafka…has been subjected to a mass ravishment by no less than three armies of interpreters. Those who read Kafka as a social allegory see case studies of the frustrations and insanity of modern bureaucracy and its ultimate issuance in the totalitarian state. Those who read Kafka as a psycho-analytic allegory see desperate revelations of Kafka's fear of his father, his castration anxieties, his sense of his own impotence, his thraldom to his dreams. Those who read Kafka as a religious allegory explain that K. in *The Castle* is trying to gain access to heaven, that Joseph K. in *The Trial* is being judged by the inexorable and mysterious justice of God.

> S. Sontag, *Against Interpretation*, Ed. David Lodge, *20th Century Literary Criticism*, p656

Apart from the main areas outlined by Sontag above, Kafka's work has been explored and analyzed in terms of history and biography. Commentators on Kafka become passionate on their stance, as Frederick Karl demonstrates:

> This and other scenes [referring to *The Trial*] have led … some critics … to argue that the focus of the novel is not Joseph K. but the proceedings; and that in *Before the Law* the central figure is the Doorkeeper…not the man from the country. This is an example of how criticism when divorced from biography can lose its way.

> F. Karl, *Franz Kafka, Representative Man*, p518n

Theorists have become very precious over their views of Kafka.

Divorcing Kafka from the text – taking the cult of personality away from the words – frees it up for a broader examination. It is true that Kafka hewed his writing from the bedrock of his personality and it is almost impossible to view wholly in isolation but when it is, the text stands by itself raising questions about the world it reflects. The events of *In The Penal Colony* or the experience of Joseph K. in *The Trial* explore ideas about the world in general as much as they reflect Kafka.

Kafka, writing in his time, was at the heart of a cultural paradigm shift and the rise of literary genres, specifically **Modernism**. As he documented his world, so his world was caught in the huge changes happening in the first half of the twentieth century.

> ## KEYWORD
>
> **Modernism:** Artistic movement concerned with the changing modern world at the end of the nineteenth and beginning of the twentieth centuries. It explored man in a rapidly changing world and man's reaction to it. Exponents include James Joyce, T. S. Eliot and Virginia Woolf.

MODERNISM, EXPRESSIONISM AND THE FANTASTIC

...Kafka seemed, of all the moderns, the most relevant, his strangely gothicized and psychological forms the most useful, his extreme inner exile the most telling of prophecies.

M. Bradbury, *The Modern British Novel 1878–2001*, p208

Kafka, writing at the beginning of the century, was in the thick of Modernism. Even though the images in the texts are quite timeless, never being identified with a specific time or place, the mind-set of the writing does place it in the realm of Modernism; exploring a feel of isolation in a rapidly changing world that wrenches control from the individual.

The Modernists who followed after World War I were more noticeable for their pessimism and their sense of a failed, fragmented society, in which the uncomprehending individual was swallowed up by huge forces outside of personal control...Such examples are, arguably, evident in...the paranoid visions of Franz Kafka...

P. Childs, *Modernism*, (Routledge 2000), p27

The powers that swept through Europe left more than the soldiers shell-shocked. Kafka reflects this in his work. The paranoia of *The Burrow* or the conflicts in *In The Penal Colony* helps bear this out.

Through accident and design, the texts of Kafka embody the emotions of existing in a shifting world. The sense of impending storms fills Kafka's work and picks up on the unease his environment must have caused. In one sense, this is only the background. In his essay *The Ideology of Modernism*, Georg Lukács says: '...Kafka and Musil [Austrian novelist] [use] the Hapsburg Monarchy, as the locus for their masterpieces. But the locus they lovingly depict is little more than a backcloth; it is not basic to their artistic intention.' (G. Lukács, *The Ideology of Modernism*, Ed. D. Lodge, *20th Century Literary Criticism*, p477).

Apart from Modernism, the other artistic movement, an extension of Modernism, with which Kafka is identified is **Expressionism**. Kafka's world of shadows fitted well with the dark feel of Expressionist painting – the antithesis of Impressionism – and the German Expressionist films of the 1920s. Peter Childs makes the claim that: 'Passages of [James] Joyce's *Ulysses*, especially the 'Nighttown' section, and [Virginia] Woolf's *The Waves* (1931) are reminiscent of Expressionist techniques, but Franz Kafka (1883–1924) is the most famous European Expressionist novelist.' (P. Childs, *Modernism*, (Routledge 2000), p119.)

Kafka's vision fitted well with the ideas and ideals of Modernism and Expressionism. This vision, dark and menacing, helped inform the images used by Expressionism and, later, in the field of **Fantastic literature**:

> According to [Jean-Paul] Sartre, [Maurice] Blanchot and Kafka no longer try to depict extraordinary beings; for them, 'there is only one fantastic object: man. Not the man of religions and spiritualisms, only half committed to the world of the body, but man-as-given, man-as-nature, man-as-society, the man who takes off his hat when a hearse passes, who kneels in churches, who marches behind a flag.' The 'normal' man is precisely the fantastic being; the fantastic becomes the rule, not the exception.'

> T. Todorov, *The Fantastic: A Structural Approach to a Literary Genre*, (Cornell University Press 1975), p173

For Todorov, Kafka's work thus becomes a focus for understanding the modern man struggling with his world. The shift in modern concerns from the outer to the inner concerns of humanity, as in the shift from

KEY TERMS

Expressionism: Artistic movement in Germany at the beginning of the twentieth century. It sought to express emotions rather than an external reality. Exponents of the genre include the painters Edvard Munch, Oskar Kokoshka and the film-maker Robert Wiene. They each used symbolism, exaggeration and distortion to convey their themes.

Fantastic literature: Literature that explores unreality in terms of a 'real' world. Exponents of this genre include Edgar Allan Poe and Nikolai Gogol. Connected to but not to be confused with fairy-tales, fantasy or science fiction.

Modernism to Post-Modernism, brings Kafka's work within the reaches of modern philosophy and psychoanalytical theory.

A PSYCHOANALYTICAL APPROACH

Martin Greenberg, in his essay *Art and Dreams*, draws a strong comparison between Kafka and Sigmund Freud:

> Kafka's subjective world of apparent irrationality hiding a heart of meaning is Freudian through and through. His literal and mythopoetic quality is Freudian. His conception of the dream is in the larger sense the same as Freud's; both understood it as an expression of unconscious experience. Kafka was preternaturally self-absorbed and, Freud or no Freud, would have lived in his own subjectivity and dreams.'

> M. Greenberg, *Art and Dreams*, Ed. H. Bloom, *Modern Critical Views: Franz Kafka*, p71

As we have seen, Gregor Samsa could be a symbol for the psyche of the Samsa family rather than a physically 'real' son. Equally, if you take Kafka's protagonists as the only 'real' characters and the people they interact with as mere manifestations of the protagonists' unconscious, then we are presented with a new perspective of Kafka's work and the quests that are central to his writing. For instance, if *The Trial* were but a dream, then everything that happens to Joseph K. would be created from his subconscious.

Another example is in *The Judgement*. Georg, looked at from a psychoanalytical point of view, has, through repression, '…no real basis for his existence anymore, and he has therefore become nearly like a marionette adapting himself to the economic and social terms of his surroundings' (L. Eilittä, *Approaches to Personal Identity in Kafka's Short Fiction*, (The Finnish Academy of Science and Letters, 1999), p87).

By looking at the text in this way, the ending becomes more comprehensible in terms of Georg's psyche – the whole scenario is built around Georg's self-condemnation rather than that of the father.

With *The Metamorphosis*, the situation that Gregor experiences is created by the way he views himself in terms of his family and the world about him: 'Gregor's transformation into an insect could be understood therefore as a regression into an infantile state where his animal body symbolizes his Oedipal fear of his father.' (L. Eilittä, op cit), p133.)

The physical transformation thus becomes symbolic of the protagonist's mind-set. Looking at this **Oedipal** view and the psychodynamics of parent–child relationships, it can be said that Gregor has actually become the 'insect' that he believes his father sees him as.

Trapped into making it worse

Throughout Kafka's fiction the protagonists seem psychologically ill-equipped to deal with their situations yet muster all they can to do so. At worst, they make things more intransigent, as in *The Trial*. At best, they gain a point of stasis, as in *The Castle*, or escape their situation by death, as in *The Hunger Artist* or in *The Metamorphosis*. The philosopher **Kierkegaard** comments on this when he says he 'envisages

> ## KEY TERMS
>
> Oedipal: The Oedipal Complex is a theory developed by Sigmund Freud whereby the son is attracted to the mother and resents the presence of the father. It is based on the Greek myth, where Oedipus unknowingly kills his father and marries his mother.
>
> Kierkegaard, Søren (1813–55): Danish philosopher. Anticipated Existentialism with philosophical works on moral responsibility and freedom of choice.

man as caught in the dilemma of wanting to comprehend Divinity with the altogether inadequate tools of rationality' (H. Czermak, *Kafka: Life and Background*, (Lincoln 1996), p10).

Kafka's texts capture this notion. Joseph K. is on a very steep learning curve in *The Trial*, and Gregor has to adapt his mind-set to accommodate his transformation. Often Kafka's heroes become snared in the web of their situation both in actuality and psychologically.

Kohlenbach suggests that often Kafka's protagonists seem to be caught in a double bind:

...one person holds the other, calling out 'go away'. The person caught in this double bind is prevented from following the verbal instruction 'go' by the physical act of being held back, which, when verbalized, results in the opposite instruction 'stay!' Whatever he does or does not do, he seems to be in the wrong.

> M. Kohlenbach, *Kafka and the German–Jewish Double Bind*, Ed. A. Hammel & E. Timms *The German–Jewish Dilemma: From Enlightenment to the Shoah*, (1999), pp177–92

In these terms what seems irrational, as with Georg's behaviour in *The Judgement*, becomes an almost inspired means of escaping the trap that has captured them. The idea of the double bind creates a no-win situation and only extreme or irrational behaviour can rescue the situation. Often, though, as with *The Castle*, the denouements of Kafka's stories seem to grind to a halt rather than finish.

KAFKA'S JEWISHNESS

Kafka is closer to the Book of Job than to what has been called 'modern literature'. His work is based on religious, and particularly Jewish, consciousness; its imitation in other contexts becomes meaningless. Kafka saw his work as an act of faith, and he did not want to be discouraging to mankind.

> J. L. Borges, *The Total Library, Non-Fiction 1922–1986*, (Penguin Books 1999), p501

Kafka is often read in terms of the Jewish religion and culture. This way of reading the texts tends to draw Kafka, the personality, back into the equation: 'Think of *the* Jewish writer, and you must think of Kafka, who evaded his own audacity, and believed nothing, and trusted only in the covenant of being a writer.' (H. Bloom, *Introduction to Modern Critical Views: Franz Kafka*, p16.)

Kafka seems to have been fairly ambivalent to Judaism, and his texts, on an initial reading, seem to have little to do with Jewishness. A closer analysis suggests a closer connection. For example, the comparison between the implement of torture in *In The Penal Colony* and ritual slaughter supports Blooms view that 'in endlessly complex ways, nearly everything Kafka wrote turns on his relation to Jews and to Jewish traditions' (H. Bloom, *The Western Canon*, p453.)

This embodiment can be related to the notion of the Jews as a persecuted race. Indeed the link between Kafka and Jewishness, and interpretations of his work in terms of God, the Old Testament and the Jewish faith, are easy to make and easy to apply. Yet dig a little deeper and studies of these religious areas become problematic and some of the applications of religious theory may seem superficial. Thus as Grozinger notes: 'The majority [of critics] either restrict themselves to vacuous generalities or else proceed from an image of Judaism that bears no resemblance whatsoever to Kafka's Jewish milieu.' (K. E. Grozinger, *Kafka and Kabbalah*, Source: www. Franz Kafka and Jewish mysticism – Kabbalah.htm).

The Kabbalah

Of all the elements of Jewishness, it is the **Kabbalah**, a branch of Jewish mysticism, that Kafka's writing is strongly associated with. Kabbalist scholar Gershom Scholem, says that: 'Although unaware of it himself, [Kafka's] writings are a secularized representation of the

KEY TERM

Kabbalah: The Jewish mystical tradition based on an esoteric interpretation of the Old Testament.

Kabbalistic conception of the world. This is why many of today's readers find something of the Absolute that breaks into pieces.' (G. Scholem, *Ten Unhistorical Statements about the Kabbalah*, (Source: www. Franz Kafka and Jewish mysticism – Kabbalah.htm).

The Kabbalah offers the student an opportunity to gain knowledge of higher realms via 'The Tree of Life'. As the body needs knowledge of the world to function properly, so the soul, in Kabbalistic terms, needs knowledge of the higher world to function properly. The Kabbalah offers an opportunity for this. Thus the similarities between Kafka and the Kabbalah can be drawn as Kafka's literature centres around his protagonists' search for knowledge to help them attain peace. Two examples of this would be Joseph K. in *The Trial* and K. in *The Castle*.

Yet, Kafka did more than use the Kabbalah as a blueprint for his concepts: 'Kafka did what many Jewish thinkers and writers before him did: he merged his Judaism with modern thinking and thus created a new form of Judaism, his own Judaism.' (K. E. Grozinger, *Kafka and Kabbalah*, Source: www. Franz Kafka and Jewish mysticism – Kabbalah.htm).

Kafka's commentary on this situation can be found in such stories as *In The Penal Colony*. Richie Robertson states that:

> What Kafka is doing in *In The Penal Colony*, then, is imagining what an organic community based on religion would be like. It would give meaning to an individual's life at the cost of extreme suffering. Yet despite its harshness, it might still be preferable to a society in which religious values would have declined and nothing but an obsession with technology has taken their place.

> R. Robertson, *Antizionismus, Zionismus: Kafka's Response to Jewish Nationalism*, Ed. J.P. Stern & J.J. White, *Paths and Labyrinths – Nine Papers from a Kafka Symposium* (Institute of Germanic Studies, W.S. Maney & Son 1985), p33

It is as if Kafka's work conveys the philosophy of the Kabbalah in the form of an extended aphorism.

MARXIST INTERPRETATIONS
For many readers, especially those who lived under extreme regimes, Kafka's work represented a 'real' world. Rather than presenting a psychological or esoteric world, his writing became representative of a world that *actually* existed. The action of Kafka's writing was realistic as opposed to metaphorical.

Capitalism
The institutions of power are often portrayed by Kafka as harsh and heartless, as, for example, in *Amerika*. According to Peter Heller, the Marxist critic, Wilheim Emric:

…interpreted the fragmentary novel, which Brod entitled *Amerika*, as a critique of the frantic, ruthlessly competitive world of work, as a denunciation of that mechanized, enslaved and enslaving industrial society which grinds us all to dust in its inexorable economic and psychological mechanisms.

P. Heller '*Up in the Gallery*': *Incongruity and Alienation*, Ed. H. Bloom, *Modern Critical Views: Franz Kafka*, p88

Amerika presents itself easily for Marxist commentary on Western capitalism. Yet, Kafka's texts never provide solutions to counter the effects of this system.

Kafka, in Marxist terms, thus appears, according to Richter, as an 'apologist for the petty bourgeoisie.' Kafka's work may have critiqued the capitalist world but generally fails to provide solutions to the problems it represents. For the Soviet Regime that banned Kafka's work, that was a heinous crime.

PHILOSOPHICAL READINGS

Because of the nature of his work – the study of man and man's situation in the world – Kafka has attracted much philosophical analysis. In particular, Kafka's texts have been linked to the work of both Søren Kierkegaard and **Frederich Nietzsche**.

> **KEY TERM**
>
> Nietzsche, Frederich (1844–1900): German philosopher. Noted for his invention of the 'superman' and his rejection of Christianity and God.

In a statement by Willy Haas:

Kafka goes back…to Kierkegaard as well as to [Blaise] Pascal; one may call him the only legitimate heir of these two. In all three there is an excruciatingly harsh basic religious theme: man is always in the wrong before God.

P. Heller '*Up in the Gallery*': *Incongruity and Alienation*, Ed. H. Bloom, *Modern Critical Views: Franz Kafka*, p90

The work of Kierkegaard looked at the relation of thought to reality and helped pave the way towards **Existentialism**. Kafka's work reflects the Existentialist philosophy by the way it focuses upon the predicament of the individual, seeing him as powerless and unable to control his own destiny.

> **KEY TERM**
>
> Existentialism: A philosophy that manifests the world from the point of the self. It suggests that we live in a meaningless world and that we are in some way trapped within our own existence.

Within Kafka's work there are numerous examples of the indiscriminate and inexplicable uses of power. Kafka's protagonists struggle within systems of power that lie beyond their comprehension. Erich Heller, in his essay 'The Castle', makes the following comparison between Kafka and Nietzsche:

> If Nietzsche's *Übermensch* is the visionary counterweight to the weight of the curse, then Kafka is its chosen victim. What sometimes has been interpreted as signs of a religious 'breakthrough' in his later writings is merely the all-engulfing weariness of a Nietzschean Prometheus: in the fourth of his Prometheus legends (Fourth Octavio Notebook) Kafka writes: '…everyone grew weary of the meaningless affair. The Gods grew weary, the eagles grew weary, the wound closed wearily.' Thus Kafka's work, as much as Nietzsche's, must remain a stumbling block to the analyzing interpreter to whom, in the enlightened atmosphere of modernity, the word 'curse' comes only as a faint memory of Greek tragedy…
>
> E. Heller, *The Castle*, Ed. H. Bloom, *Modern Critical Views: Franz Kafka*, p138

Nietzsche's endlessly questioning philosophy finds a resonance in Kafka's fiction. Both have examined the values of morality and a belief in God. Whereas Kafka's fictional world appears Godless, Nietzsche pronounced that 'God was dead'.

OTHER VIEWS OF KAFKA

> As there is a Fortress Freud so there is a Fortress Kafka, Kafka his own castle. For admission a certain high seriousness must be deemed essential and I am not sure I have it.

> A. Bennett, *Alan Bennett Plays 2*, (Faber and Faber 1998), p3

This being said, Bennett did go on and write two plays loosely based around the life of Kafka – *Kafka's Dick* and *The Insurance Man*. Even though Bennett thought himself not high-brow enough to deal with Kafka, he, nonetheless, felt comfortable enough to write about or around him.

Kafka raises more questions than he answers. His texts embody many issues that are of concern today. Kafka is not only fascinating to academics but he is also fascinating for individuals and other artists. Creative minds seem to be drawn to Kafka and use him for inspiration; his work connects with the individual and this is possibly why many writers and artists identify with his work. The playwright, actor and director Steven Berkoff, in the introduction to his theatrical transcription of *The Trial* says:

> Kafka expressed me as I expressed Kafka. His words stung and hung on my brain, infused themselves in my art and were regurgitated in my work. The labyrinth. The endless puzzle or the myth of Sisyphus, the quest of Theseus through the maze. Was I Theseus? Joseph K's mediocrity was mine and his ordinariness and fears were mine too: the 'under-hero' struggling to find the ego that would lead him to salvation.'

> S. Berkoff, *The Trial*, (Amber Lane Press 1988), p5

The film director David Lynch, whose film *Blue Velvet* was described by J.G. Ballard as 'the *Wizard of Oz* reshot with a script by Franz Kafka', says of Kafka: 'Some of his things are the most thrilling combos of words I have ever read. If Kafka wrote a crime picture, I'd be there. I'd like to direct that for sure.' (D. Lynch, Ed. Chris Rodley, *Lynch on Lynch*, (Faber and Faber 1997), p56.)

We see in Lynch an example of the passion that Kafka raises in other writers. Kafka's work champions the outsider and many creative talents find themselves able to empathize with the alienation and disempowerment of the individual which his work evokes.

That being said, not all who have dabbled with Kafka's words speak highly of the writer. The director Orson Welles, who wrote and directed the 1963 film version of *The Trial*, said dismissively: 'I do not share Kafka's point of view in *The Trial*. I believe he is a good writer, but Kafka is not the extraordinary genius that people today see in him.' (Orson Welles on his film version of *The Trial*, Source: Leni's Franz Kafka Page.)

Kafka, the man, seems to attract film-makers as much as his writing does. The director Steven Soderbergh made *Kafka* (1991), a fantasy loosely based on the life of Kafka and Peter Capaldi made a charming, Oscar®-winning short film in 1995 called *Franz Kafka's It's A Wonderful Life*. With these examples, the film-makers turn Kafka into his own fiction. Kafka becomes one of his own characters.

✳ ✳ ✳SUMMARY ✳ ✳ ✳

• Kafka is regarded as a Modernist and Expressionist writer.

• Kafka's work can be interpreted in terms of psychoanalytical theory, religion, politics or Existential philosophy.

• Many commentators are equally fascinated by Kafka the man as well as Kafka's work.

• Kafka is seen as important for the individual with individual interpretations as well as the prescribed interpretations of more formal theoretical analysis.

Where To Next?

KAFKA'S WORK

Nearly every scrap of Kafka's work that still exists is readily available on bookshop shelves and has never gone out of print. There should be no problem in getting your hands on his fiction, either in separate volumes or in collections. These are generally found in the Penguin or Vintage imprint, although there are plenty of other publishers that produce his work in print. The main American publisher of Kafka's work is Schocken. Because Kafka never produced a huge amount of fiction, his collected works should be available in no more than a couple of volumes. *The Penguin Complete Short Stories of Franz Kafka*, for instance, only runs to 500 pages!

Kafka's diaries are collected together in one volume, as too are *Letters to Felice* and *Letters to Milena*. These volumes are published by Vintage Classics. Also available are his *Blue Octavio Notebooks* which contain *Reflections on Sin, Suffering, Hope and the True Way*. This is published by Exact Change publishers. *Letter to Father* (or *Dearest Father*) is also available from the same publishers. His work is also widely available from Czech and German publishers as well, many in an English translation.

Since he laid his life bare in obvious and exaggerated ways within all forms of his writing, there is plenty from the man himself to give you an insight into one of the most influential writer's of the twentieth century.

BIOGRAPHY

There are a good few biographies of Kafka available. An obvious choice would be from Kafka's long-time friend and editor Max Brod. This biography, *Franz Kafka*, originally published in 1937, is still in print and available from Da Capo Press. This is a very personal view so is probably not as neutral as other biographies.

A hefty biography, *Franz Kafka, Representative Man, Prague, Germans, Jews and the Crisis of Modernism*, by Frederick Karl and published by Fromm International should tell you everything you should ever need to know about Kafka. It works well as an encyclopaedia and proves useful for pinpointing specific facts and information.

A less bulky but still enlightening biography is *K: A Biography of Kafka* by Ronald Hayman, published by Phoenix Giant. This is a straightforward read with some good insights into the man.

CRITICAL WORKS

As well as being cited in books dealing with literary criticism in general, there are many books of collected criticism looking at every possible interpretation of Kafka's work. As a starting point a couple of volumes of criticism devoted directly to Kafka are worth a look. One is a collection of essays from various critics and literary commentators under the title of *Modern Critical Views: Franz Kafka*. This edition is edited by Harold Bloom and published by the American publishers Chelsea House. The book presents the reader with a wide range of views and opinions.

Another interesting book that looks at Kafka's work in a theoretical way is *Franz Kafka, The Jewish Patient* by Sander Gilman and published by Routledge. This looks at Kafka's writing from a very detailed Jewish viewpoint and is good for an overview of modern Jewish history, Jewishness in terms of culture and how Kafka's work explores or reflects the Jewish culture.

A much slimmer volume, but good for a point of reference about Kafka's work is *Franz Kafka: Life, Work and Criticism* by Kurt Fickert and published by the Canadian York Press.

For a poststructuralist view of Kafka there is Jacques Derrida's reading of Kafka's short story 'Before the Law'. Derrida reads the story as a parable about the failure of exerting one's rights through legal means. The translation of Derrida's work is published as *Dissemination* by Chicago University Press.

PRAGUE

A must for anyone particularly interested in Kafka is a visit to Prague in the Czech Republic. Since Kafka spent the majority of his life living and working in Prague, practically every cobble walked on will have been crossed by the man himself. Although the Jewish quarter is there in name only, the city still holds the atmosphere of the Prague that Kafka knew.

Most of the buildings significant to Kafka's life are still standing. There is a museum dedicated to Kafka in the house where he was born and there are Kafka walks that will guide you around his life in Prague. His little studio in Golden Lane by the imposing St. Vitas cathedral in the castle is now a tiny bookshop. There is another bookshop that has an excellent range of Kafka books in the Kinský Palace on the Old Town square as well as the Kafka Society and the Milena Café.

A good book to take around Prague is *Franz Kafka and Prague* by Harald Salfellner and produced by the Czech publisher Vitalis. This acts as a guide book around the significant Kafka sights in Prague. Despite the unfortunate start, Prague has now embraced Kafka and celebrates him. There is no shortage of Kafka t-shirts, mugs and other Kafka-related goodies on practically every street corner.

FILM

There are quite a few films and theatre productions out there with some connection to Kafka. Probably the best-known recreation of a Kafka story on celluloid is Orson Welles' interpretation of *The Trial* made in 1962. Although the story is tweaked in places, it is still worth viewing. It is a brooding film with distinctive touches by Welles. Even so, there is still the spirit of Kafka in the dark shadows.

Another film worth having a look at is the1991 film *Kafka* by Steven Soderbergh. Although more a fantasy based on Kafka as opposed to a straight biography of the writer, it does explore the essence of Kafka recreated in the mood of old German Expressionist and early Hollywood horror films.

Adaptations of *The Trial*, *The Metamorphosis* and *In The Penal Colony* have been made by Steven Berkoff for the stage, and Alan Bennett has turned his charm upon Kafka in his two plays *Kafka's Dick* and *The Insurance Man*.

SOCIETIES AND WEBSITES

There are thousands of websites connected to Kafka. Everything you should ever need to know, and many things that you don't, can be found by surfing the net. It seems that Kafka has been embraced more fully by the individual than by organizations. The web will provide a rich entrance to the phenomenon that Kafka has become. Some of sites that are worth visiting are *Joseph K's Castle Page*, *Leni's Franz Kafka Page* and *Constructing Franz Kafka*. All offer interesting information and good links to other sites.

There are plenty of websites connected to Kafka Societies and Kafka Circles in Europe and America to get involved with, as well as plentiful biographies, analysis of specific texts and curiosities. It is worth taking a browse through the web just to get a flavour of what is available – from the sublime to the absolutely absurd.

Chronology of major works

WORK PUBLISHED DURING KAFKA'S LIFETIME

1908 *Meditations,* Hyperion (No. 1, Jan–Feb p91–94)

1909 *Conversations with the Supplicant, Conversations with the Drunken Man,* Hyperion (No. 8, Mar–Apr p126–31 & p131–33)

1910 *Collected Aphorisms,* Bohemia (No. 86, March)

1913 *Meditations* (collection), Leipzig, Rowohlt

1913 *The Judgement,* Arkadia

1913 *The Stoker, A Fragment,* Leipzig, Kurt Wolff

1915 *Before the Law,* Selbstwehr (No. 34, September)

1915 *The Metamorphosis,* Die weißen Blätter (No. 10, October)

1917 *A Dream,* Prague, Das Jüdische Prag

1917 *An Old Manuscript, The New Advocate, A Fratricide,* Marsyas (No. 1, July–Aug)

1917 *Report to an academy,* Der Jude. (Oct–Nov)

1919 *In the Penal Colony,* Leipzig, Kurt Wolff

1919 *A Country Doctor* (collection), Leipzig, Kurt Wolff

1922 *The Hunger Artist,* Die neue Rundschau (October, p983–92)

1924 *Josephine the Singer,* Prager Press (No. 110, April p4–7)

1924 *The Hunger Artist* (collection), Berlin, Die Schmide

MAJOR PUBLICATIONS AFTER KAFKA'S DEATH

1925 *The Trial,* Berlin, Die Schmiede

1926 *The Castle,* München, Kurt Wolff

1927 *Amerika,* München, Kurt Wolff

1931 *The Great Wall of China* (collection), Berlin, Gustav Kiepenhauer

1936 *Description of a struggle* (collection), Prague, Heinrich Mercy Sohn

1937 *Diaries and Letters,* Prague, Heinrich Mercy Sohn

1953 *Wedding Preparations in the Country,* Frankfurt, Fischer

GLOSSARY

Allegory A story, poem or picture in which the apparent meaning of the characters or events relate to a deeper or spiritual meaning.

Aphorism A short, pithy saying expressing a general truth.

Bohemian Pertaining to Bohemia, a kingdom of central Europe. Independent from the ninth to the thirteenth centuries, it was ruled by the Hapsburgs up until 1918. It relates, mainly, to the Czech Republic and the Czech language.

Bourgeoisie The 'middle class'. In Marxist terms, the rich who oppress the workers.

Czechoslovakia A republic formed, after the fall of the Hapsburg Empire, out of the Czechs in Bohemia and Moravia and the Slovaks in Slovakia. Occupied by the Germans in 1939 and then by the Soviet Union in 1945.

Existentialism A philosophy that manifests the world from the point of the self. It suggests that we live in a meaningless world and that we are in some way trapped within our own existence.

Expressionism Artistic movement in Germany at the beginning of the twentieth century. It sought to express emotions rather than an external reality. Exponents of the genre include the painters Edvard Munch, Oskar Kokoshka and the film-maker Robert Wiene. Used symbolism, exaggeration and distortion to convey their themes.

Fantastic literature Literature that explores unreality in terms of a 'real' world. Exponents of this genre include Edgar Allan Poe and Nikolai Gogol. Connected to but not to be confused with fairy-tales, fantasy or science fiction.

Fin de siècle Relating to the changes in morals and society pertaining to the end of the nineteenth and beginning of the twentieth centuries.

Ghetto An area of a city that is segregated. It acts to isolate small populations.

Golem The traditional Jewish tale of a man made out of clay that was brought to life by a Rabbi to protect the community. The Yiddish word EMETH ('truth') is inscribed on the Golem's forehead to bring him to life (or written on parchment and placed in the Golem's mouth, depending on which version you read). Every Sabbath, the E is scratched off. The resultant word METH ('death') halts the Golem. One Sabbath the Rabbi forgets to do this and the Golem runs amok, almost annihilating the community. The Rabbi arrives and rubs away the writing thus destroying the Golem. He then teaches the community to beware – that which protects can also destroy.

Hapsburg Empire German Princely family that ruled central Europe under the auspices of the Holy Roman Empire from 1440 to 1806. They provided rulers for central Europe including Austria, Spain and Bohemia. The line continued as the house of Hapsburg-Lorraine ruling Austria from 1806 to 1848 and Austria-Hungary from 1848 until 1918 when World War I brought an end to their rule.

Kabbalah The Jewish mystical tradition based on an esoteric interpretation of the Old Testament.

KGB *Komitet Gosudarstvennoi Bezopasnosti* – the Soviet secret police.

Kierkegaard, Søren (1813–55) Danish philosopher. Anticipated Existentialism with philosophical works on moral responsibility and freedom of choice.

Kosher That which accords to Jewish law. Food that is prepared in the correct dietary way in terms of Jewish law.

Modernism Artistic movement concerned with the changing modern world at the end of the nineteenth and beginning of the twentieth centuries. It explored man in a rapidly changing world and man's reaction to it. Exponents include James Joyce, T. S. Eliot and Virginia Woolf.

Nabokov, Vladimir 1899–1977. Russian-born, American writer. Author of *Lolita*.

Nietzsche, Frederich
1844–1900. German philosopher. Noted for his invention of the 'superman' and his rejection of Christianity and God.

Oedipal The Oedipal Complex is a theory developed by Sigmund Freud whereby the son is attracted to the mother and resents the presence of the father. It is based on the Greek myth, where Oedipus unknowingly kills his father and marries his mother.

Orwellian Referring to a dehumanized, authoritarian society as described in the novel *1984*.

Parable A story that uses familiar events to portray a religious or ethical situation.

Prague Castle and St Vitas' Cathedral The castle and cathedral overlook Prague from the opposite side of the river Vltava. The buildings tower over the landscape and are one of the distinctive landmarks in the city.

Protagonist The principle character in a play or novel.

Shehitah Jewish ritual slaughter to produce Kosher meat.

Talmudic (Talmud) The primary source of Jewish religious law.

Torah The scroll used in a synagogue service that contains Jewish teaching.

Tuberculosis A communicable disease caused by *tubercle bacillus*. Most frequently attacks the lungs. Also known as consumption.

Yiddish Vernacular language spoken by European and emigrant Jews.

FURTHER READING

The Writings of Kafka

F. Kafka (trans. M. Hofmann), *The Man Who Disappeared (Amerika)*, Penguin Books, 1996

F. Kafka (trans. W. and E. Muir), *The Trial*, Penguin, 1983

F. Kafka (trans. W. and E. Muir), *The Castle*, Penguin, 1983

F. Kafka (various translators), *The Penguin Complete Short Stories of Franz Kafka*, Penguin, 1983

F. Kafka (trans. S. Mortkowitz), *Meditations*, Vitalis, 1998

F. Kafka (trans. K. Reppin), *Letter to Father*, Vitalis, 1999

F. Kafka (trans. E. Kaiser & E. Wilkins), *The Blue Octavio Notebooks*, Exact Change, 1991

Biography

J. Adler, *Illustrated Lives: Franz Kafka*, Penguin Books, 2001

M. Brod, *Franz Kafka*, Da Capo Press, 1995

R. Hayman, *K: A Biography of Kafka*, Phoenix Giant, 1988

F. Karl, *Franz Kafka, Representative Man*, Fromm International Publishing Corporation, 1993

Critical Studies

H. Bloom (ed.), *Modern Critical Views: Kafka*, Chelsea House Publishers, 1986

H. Bloom, *The Western Canon*, Papermac, 1994

M. Bradbury, *The Modern British Novel 1878–2001*, Penguin Books, 2001

M. Esslin, *The Theatre of the Absurd*, Penguin Books, 1991

K. J. Fickert, *Franz Kafka. Life, Work and Criticism*, York Press, 1984

S. Gilman, *Franz Kafka, The Jewish Patient*, Routledge, 1995

R. H. Lawson, *Franz Kafka*, Ungar, 1987

D. Lodge (ed.), *20th Century Literary Criticism*, Longman, 1972

H. Salfellner, *Franz Kafka and Prague*, Vitalis, 1998

S. Spector, *Prague Territories*, University of California Press, 2000

R. Spiers & B. Sandberg, *Franz Kafka*, MacMillan Press, 1997

INDEX